Sustainable Architecture in Japan

The Green Buildings of Nikken Sekkei

Sustainable Architecture in Japan

The Green Buildings of Nikken Sekkei

Introduction by Eiji Maki
and William A. McDonough

Edited by Anna Ray-Jones

WILEY-ACADEMY

Cover:
Lake Biwa Museum and
UNEP International
Environmental Technology
Center

First published
in Great Britain in 2000 by
Wiley-Academy
A division of
John Wiley & Sons
Baffins Lane
Chichester
West Sussex PO19 1UD

ISBN: 0471864579

Editors in Japan:
Kazuo Matsunari
Yukiko Nakada

Translator:
Matthew Kinnersly

Design collaborator in Japan:
Hiroshige Kuwahara

Design:
Willi Kunz Associates
New York

Writer/Editor:
Anna Ray-Jones, New York

Senior Editor:
Wiley-Academy
Maggie Toy

Other Wiley Editorial Offices:
New York, Weinheim,
Brisbane, Singapore, Toronto

Printed and bound in Italy

Acknowledgements

Nikken Sekkei is deeply appreciative of the many people who gave their time and skills to the creation of this book. We express immense gratitude to our clients for providing us with the opportunity to create their projects based on the values of sustainable design. Their understanding of this kind of building design has allowed us to expand and contribute our knowledge to an essential and growing revolutionary movement in global architecture.

We give great respect and thanks to our scientific and academic consultants whose wisdom is presented in Part III of this book. We are proud to name them as our colleagues: Masanori Shukuya, Dr. Eng., Professor, Faculty of Environmental and Information Studies and the Graduate School of Architecture, Musashi Institute of Technology; Shin-ichi Tanabe, Ph.D., Associate Professor, Department of Architecture Waseda University; Shuzo Murakami, Dr. Eng., Professor, Institute of Industrial Science, University of Tokyo; Akira Hoyano, Dr. Eng., Professor, Graduate School, Tokyo Institute of Technology; Yoh Matsuo, Dr. Eng., Professor Emeritus, the University of Tokyo; Tatsuya Inooka, General Manager of Environmental Engineering Group at Nikken Sekkei Osaka; Koichi Kaiho, Senior Engineer, Nikken Sekkei Tokyo; Toshiharu Ikaga, Associate Professor, Institute of Industrial Science, University of Tokyo. These renowned scholars and engineers have been a wonderful source of scientific research and data for many of Nikken Sekkei's buildings, advising and collaborating on key aspects of energy systems as they relate to sustainable design.

We are grateful for the insights and the participation of William A. McDonough of McDonough & Partners, USA, an American architect whose first home was Japan. Although our architectural firms practise on opposite sides of the world, McDonough & Partners affirms our pursuit of sustainable architecture as a universal goal.

This publication would not have been possible without the dedication and excellent direction provided by G by K Co., Ltd, who acted as the Japanese publishing coordinator of the project, in particular, Kazuo Matsunari, Hiroshige Kuwahara, Yukiko Nakada and Matthew Kinnersly.

To our colleagues in the USA, we give special recognition and thanks to Willi Kunz of Willi Kunz Associates and writer/editor, Anna Ray-Jones, a team whose continuing commitment and tireless efforts brought the book to completion. To Academy editor, Maggie Toy and her staff, and to John Wiley & Sons UK, for publishing this collection of Nikken Sekkei's sustainable designs, we also offer our deep gratitude.

Contents

Sustainable Architecture: An East–West Perspective

Eiji Maki
Nikken Sekkei, Japan

and

William A. McDonough
William A. McDonough & Partners, USA

Eiji Maki

Architecture and Energy Saving

The vision and skill of the modern architect, no matter where they practise, essentially operate in a global context. The design of cities and buildings worldwide contributes to the health or detriment of the earth's environment. Their environmental impact is not just localized, but extends across oceans, polar points and atmospheric layers. Given the inter-connections of these effects, it's the architect's primary responsibility to design buildings that are energy saving and protective of natural resources. This is an important principle at Nikken Sekkei and has been an integral part of our design protocols for many years. We have endeavoured to achieve energy-saving results by various design strategies, such as improving the envelope structure of buildings (utilizing outside stress shutoff by heat insulation and eaves) in the early stages of a project, and enhancing the efficiency of air conditioning, lighting and load carriage in equipment planning.

Today, users of buildings, whether in the home or the workspace, require immediate comfort and convenience. This has led to an increased demand for energy in both the domestic and industrial sector, and we find ourselves in a situation where energy saving has never been so critical. Relevant regulations in Japan (such as PAL and CEC values) have become increasingly stringent. In order to implement permanent energy-saving measures, it is crucial to determine and control the energy consumption in a building precisely. Technology for this purpose is also very important. However, energy-saving technology in sustainable design is a constantly evolving process.

What is state-of-the art today is quickly subsumed by tomorrow's new innovations as we discover more refined solutions to energy conservation and environmental problems. Over the years, I have closely followed the latest thinking on new and emerging technologies and have been able to integrate many new systems and materials into the design of several Nikken Sekkei buildings. I am positive that further progress will be made in innovative systems and new materials that save and recover energy.

Architecture and Global Environmental Problems

The concept of architecture existing in harmony with nature is not a new idea. In the course of searching for vital indoor space, effective energy use and a sound global environment, we in Japan find ourselves revisiting our old ways of thinking about buildings (just as architects have in other ecologically compromised regions). The amity between site and building, between the exterior wall and the forested perimeter, is an ancient collaboration. Throughout the traditions of Japanese architecture, the function and form of buildings, from the woodcutter's hut to great temples, has always been meshed with the natural world. The notion of nature as an alien force that needs to be kept away from the built space, is a concept originating from industrial expansion. The elements were always allowed access in classical Japanese houses, gently channelled by simple, elegant design whereby the building became an ally in the harnessed expressions of wind and sun. These spaces allowed the dweller to experience soft light filtered through shoji screens and cool breezes that travelled freely from porch to porch.

While the past recedes from us, the success of traditional design strategies is a rich legacy that holds many solutions for the practice of sustainable architecture. As the reader will discover in Part II of this book, Nikken Sekkei has drawn from this unique heritage. We have taken certain traditional architectural innovations, reinterpreted them in new materials, new control systems and integrated them into many of our current projects. However, transforming building traditions so that they can be applied appropriately to modern design requires our understanding of a whole range of complex challenges that never existed in the past.

Our cities worldwide are plagued with the hazards of global warming, ozone layer destruction and acid rain, caused by the over-consumption of energy and other natural resources. Such dilemmas can be offset by using less energy in innovative ways. To achieve this, it's necessary to clarify how building operations affect the global environment at each stage of a building's 'lifetime'. From this viewpoint, an analysis should be made during 'life cycle assessments'. Simultaneously, it is necessary to radically review the building's interior planning. In modern buildings, because efficiency has long been such a dictate, space construction in relation to lighting and thermal control is now flat and devoid of variation per hour. As architects, we are compelled to ask what is a healthy and vital built space for human beings? How can it be realized in architecture and also have a benign effect on its surroundings? In this book, we are proposing some answers to these important questions by presenting several of our major sustainable projects built with maximum utilization of new technology and materials. This is our direction in achieving an architecture that exists in harmony with the environment.

From 'Shielding' to Reconciliation with Nature

In our introspection on sustainable architecture, we find that the conventions of building design have changed over time, from shutting off the outer environment to protect the inside, to folding nature and natural energy into the plan (as was the case with traditional Japanese architecture). For example, consider our reinterpretation of deep eaves and 'shoji' screens (made of special glass), both of which are traditional architectural features suitable to the Japanese climate and terrain. At the International Institute for Advanced Studies, we designed glass 'shoji' and arranged them around the windows to disperse natural light, transforming it into a soft, comfortable 'lighting'. However, traditional architectural methods cannot be applied easily or indiscriminately to people accustomed to environmental consistency or to high-rise buildings and buildings that generate a tremendous amount of heat. Furthermore, the present-day global environment, social conditions and problems with the in-house environment contain too many variables that cannot be answered simply by returning to traditional architectural forms. We need to develop means of adapting new systems and materials combined with the latest advanced analysis methods for buildings that are designed to exist appropriately with modern demands.

The Current Challenges of Environmental Architecture

Air conditioning, lighting and other mechanical systems are highly developed technologies that have enormously benefited both dwellers and architects, giving them a scope of freedom and physical comfort unprecedented in our history. However, we question whether people's life styles and architecture's outer structure depend too heavily and blindly on such systems. As a result of our excessive dependence on mechanical systems and wanton energy consumption, environmental destruction has been accelerated. We are all too familiar with the standardized, tasteless, lifeless and unhealthy architecture that abounds in every modern city on the globe. This excess and indifference is often reflected in contemporary building design. In our quest for the optimal human environment we must cease using all advanced technology for further system development alone. It is high time that we mandated the active use of such technologies to create a totally new kind of affinity between architecture and machinery. This would open the way for the design of more lively living spaces, and possibly to a breakthrough in energy-saving methods. Energy conservation seems to have hit a ceiling because the outer structure of buildings and their operating technologies have been developed separately (although this has admittedly achieved remarkable effects).

At Nikken Sekkei, we have strived for such results for many years. This book introduces some of our attempts: natural ventilation using an 'air flow roof' at RITE that we designed; air conditioning by 'night time purge' and beneath-the-floor blowout at Panasonic Multimedia Centre; natural ventilation and light control at Tokyo Gas Company's Earth Port. These buildings have innovative features that utilize the intake of natural energy and resources, solar heat/light, wind, geothermal energy and rainwater. Also adopted therein are various mechanical energy-saving methods and new energy systems that combine to reduce adverse effects upon the environment.

Beyond Reconciliation with Nature

When an architect regularly designs buildings that have 'amity with the environment' they inevitably encounter one problem after another: is such a building really possible in the midst of a busy city plagued by traffic congestion, the hustle-and-bustle of too many people, air pollution and noise? The location is, I believe, critical to buildings that are designed for sustainability. In designing for natural ventilation, one is faced with the problems of ambient noise, heat and dust. While the builder must take these issues into consideration, the foremost priority for any building that is environmentally beneficial is to ensure that the site is suitable to the design. And in turn, for such an environment to realize and support buildings that have an 'amity with Nature', such concepts and requirements must prevail in densely populated centres. Soil, natural growth and water surfaces in most cities and urban areas have for decades been covered over and sealed with concrete and asphalt. This has brought about the heat island phenomenon. Heat has accelerated the use of air coolers in buildings, which has further aggravated the phenomenon. It is a vicious cycle, which must be stopped if we are to prevent environmental hazards and improve the quality, not just of our air and water, but of our lives and those of future generations. As a matter of course, such problems present many economic, social and technical issues to be solved. As architects and designers in search of answers, we must face and discuss such issues in continuing dialogue with each other and professionals from related disciplines. It's essential that we restore water and green spaces in cities. The Osaka Municipal Central Gymnasium is an example of our efforts to bring such spaces back to crowded city centres. New buildings should use and match such 'soft' areas to adjust and enhance residential space environmentally. There should also be a networking of buildings and facilities so that residents of one building may share the benefits of another in order to create a sustainable urban environment. This kind of building design, its integral values, and the quality of the environment it sustains should be handed down over generations. We, as architects and engineers, hope to contribute whatever we can to such a grand scheme.

The Architect's Attitude

A fundamental factor in making our architectural processes sustainable is the attitude and intention adopted by the design team. It's essential that the team be unified in the practice and execution of the project on a daily basis from the very early stages. Unless close cooperation is established from the beginning and maintained firmly among the client, architect, structure designer, environment planner and other related professionals, they can hardly realize a building with real 'amity with the environment'. We must also be aware that mere casual ideas will not work, and that the design must be backed with solid, proven technology. In other words, an architect who proposes a new approach to the design must simulate its features, accomplish the data and provide results, repeat and confirm the design's efficacy to prove that its environmental elements and measures will be effective. It's required of the senior architect and their design team to be in unison and present an improved idea, practise it and again confirm its effects in real building work(s). It is a cyclical process of projection, practice and verification. Throughout the process, we evaluate our own architectural systems by using mathematical analyses and other techniques. Such evaluations maintain our continuing collaboration and interaction with academics and researchers, and refine our professional skills. If we are to build some construction as a solution to multi-faceted environmental problems in our own age, the achievements of such collective, multidisciplinary work will take on and play a greater role in the realization of our buildings. A number of research papers appearing in Part III of this book are from specialized fields where we contributed to the total work. Another challenge to environmental design quality is frequently the project's financial planning. For any building to be truly sustainable, costs—both the initial and operating expenses—must be regarded and thought through clearly. This is another important key in order that sustainable architectural designs prevail.

Nikken Sekkei has been designing buildings in Japan and elsewhere for almost a hundred years. In this long and durable history, we have practised our skills throughout every changing phase of our nation's architecture, making significant contributions to the development of materials, design concepts and helping to change the face of the Japanese city and our urban landscape. One might say that Nikken Sekkei has grown alongside this special century in Japan that has brought forth tremendous economic growth and new technologies. These intense and rapid changes have also impacted our environment with serious consequences that challenge us, as architects and engineers, to find appropriate and positive solutions. Indeed, seeking answers to environmental problems has been a creative force in our designs and has stimulated us to reassess the long-term purpose and effects of our buildings, their adaptability, their longevity and the mechanisms and materials that we utilize.

Now we stand at the brink of a new century, a pivotal point in the continuum of Nikken Sekkei's architecture. When we look back we see a repertoire of buildings, linked from decade to decade by invention and innovation.

As we look forward, we are mindful that it is our obligation as architects to meet the future with a full understanding that sustainable architecture must become the commonplace in design, and not the exception. And that we are ultimately responsible for the wellbeing of not only our buildings and building users, but the very fabric of nature and the environment.

William A. McDonough

I was born in Japan (my parents were American residents in Tokyo). My first home was a classical Japanese house and we lived there very much in the Japanese manner. I remember lying on the floor on my futon, staring at the ceiling and noticing how all the beams came together. I recall sitting on the verandah overlooking a highly formal but serenely beautiful garden with secluded ponds—very fascinating to a small boy. The house always had the particularly pungent scent of warm cedar. The space was utterly flexible and easily adaptable for a variety of human uses. I remember it being open, cool and tranquil. My strongest image is that it was a house without walls, and that we seemed to be living in a perpetual pavilion.

I've always had a predilection for the kind of buildings I'm designing now. While I was a student at Yale, I built Ireland's first active-solar heated house. I learned a great deal from the project and it became a turning point to a particular direction. I had grown up in Japan, which is a sort of rarefied world. It taught me ways to engage with and delight in elegant objects of very subtle design. It's a question of scale and the continuum of the aesthetic. In Japan, you find a consistent appreciation for the beauty of harmonious design and precise spatial relationships, for the importance of mindfulness, of timelessness. These values are built into the very fabric of their traditional buildings. I thought then that such aesthetics were common to everyday life, everywhere. However, when I came to the United States, I found myself in the thick of a consumer society where aesthetics took a back seat and people had lifestyles instead of lives. This was certainly evident in the design of buildings and American cities in the 1950s and 60s. My progress toward a deeply informed and sustaining architecture comes from a desire to return to the human and natural aesthetic, to celebrate that which is mindful, harmonious and sustaining. This is reflected in our practice today. As designers and thinkers we've been working to move the sustainability agenda forward with our client base. Most of what William McDonough & Partners designs incorporates sustainable features as much as possible. One thing that differentiates us from many architectural firms is that we're designing from the level of the molecule up to the region.

What I find interesting in the work of Nikken Sekkei is that it's very focused and highly inventive as sustainable commercial, domestic and institutional architecture. Their link with their nation's design heritage is a pure lineage that remains unbroken. If you study traditional Japanese architecture closely, you find in their ancient technique very sophisticated methods of amalgamating mass and membrane. The Japanese people evolved ways to deal with solid materials full of thermal capacity to store heat as a building cools. They also utilized 'resistance' methods, using thatched roofs, porches and shingled walls and shoji screens. The material history of their architecture is based on the intricate interaction of membrane, mass, and resistant surfaces. If you look at their techniques and materials, what they were doing, with respect to the Japanese climate, was insulating the building's user from the extremes of weather. However, Nikken Sekkei's contemporary designs are dealing with a whole new set of parameters that essentially arose out of glass technologies. Along with modern architecture came the large sheet of glass, and the abundance of cheap energy. All of a sudden, architects seem to forget where the sun is, and they start using glass, which early modernists thought would connect people to nature, only now it's being utilized in ways that totally seal people up in boxes. Architects using this approach evidence their disconnection from the fundamental flows of nature.

The true assignment of modern architecture is to integrate glazing with the traditional wisdom, using 'capacity' and 'resistance insulation', and how to find new forms of cultural expression using local materials engaged with the local climate around the way people really live. If we really use this book and the marvellous work it describes as a launching pad for thought, we recognize that what we're seeing is transparency integrated with traditional technique. This allows us to take stock of our own design protocols. The green architecture of Nikken Sekkei is a major part of a great global manifestation of sustainable design. Their presence on the international architectural stage, and the body of work they've achieved, allows us to review where we were, where we could be now, and how we might chart a new course. The hallmarks of their strategy of change are world-class and make a very convincing display of how it's possible to effect change. It challenges the existing system by allowing it to be less bad and opens the possibility of building on the results toward a new direction.

In my design firm we address our strategy as sustaining and the goal we've set ourselves is trying to reach 100% sustainable. That's the difference—which is our creative agenda. However, we have to be humble in this attitude because, you see, they may be right in some cases, and we may be right in others. Nikken Sekkei's trajectory is somewhat different from our own, we are working on different fronts; gathering answers for similar design issues and concerns. There is a power in this, especially if we share the information. Our trajectory celebrates nature's fecundity and abundance. It seeks to transform environmental menaces into processes and materials that can extend the productivity of a building.

To change the current scenario in modern architecture, we need to understand how we can extend the implications of the direction that's being charted in this book. I find work that's presented in these pages an heroic approach. What they've achieved is more imaginative than they even realize. If you take a look at their sports hall, the Osaka Gymnasium—how many buildings do you know in the USA have made oxygen lately? A sports arena is often designed to be one of the most aggressive buildings in the world. Here, it turns out to be a little green hill, and it's covered with growing things that make oxygen. It's got multiple benefits. It's people-friendly and life enhancing. It's brilliant, this is a really smart building. I'd like to honour the architects of Nikken Sekkei by saying what they're allowing to happen is a new strategy of change that we, in our practice, call 'eco-effectiveness'.

What is actually called for in modern architecture is a re-evolution; some term it the next industrial revolution, but it's actually a re-evolution. Darwin was misinterpreted, because everyone thought he said survival of the fittest, when what he meant was survival of the most fitting in their niche. Nature is not necessarily more efficient than some styles of architecture; however, it does create optimum conditions and mechanisms for survival that are self-sustaining and constantly re-innovated. The question becomes 'can modern architecture mirror this kind of creative flexibility, this ultimate adaptability that is so essential for life to move forward?' Nature's evolutionary agenda allows for more and more niches, more fecundity, and increasing diversity. Then along come humans with our first Industrial Revolution and guess what? Modern design is about eliminating all of that. It's one-size-fits-all thinking. However, sustainable design runs counterpoint to this narrow mindset. It calls for a return to considering buildings as heterogeneous, as having a correct sense of place, of fitting into their environmental niche and interacting with their locale appropriately.

From our own design approach, we're actually going deeper into the molecule. Together with our colleague, Michael Braungart, we're designing chemicals, fibres and building materials that are environmentally nurturing from their inception. What we're trying to do at William McDonough & Partners and McDonough Braungart Design Chemistry is to address both the molecular and the regional scale and integrate the results into our architecture. Our buildings and products are designed either into the biological system or into the technical system. It's our imperative to create products and materials that will recycle back to industry, safely and intelligently.

In contrast, the work of Nikken Sekkei is a manifestation of sustainable design at a certain scale. It's at the scale of the house, the institutional building, the office building, sports arena. It works from the domestic scale to the institutional scale. Nikken Sekkei have all the signals that we need in their approach. They talk about design for disassembly. They've hit the main point exactly. They have perfected the right language for how to think about a building that needs to be able to come apart easily, especially in a culture that's moving so fast. Japan creates major buildings and tears them down frequently.

Nikken Sekkei has the idea that they could design for long-term value and ultimately reverse this scenario. We too believe that the longevity of buildings and their parts is an intrinsic green principle. This requires design for adapting and reusing the building, such as offices to apartments and vice versa, and planning for reusing materials generated by the building's demolition. Our mutual architectural trajectories meet in many areas. Their methods on how to store water, cool buildings with water, create natural energy zones, integrate mass and membrane with transparency, deal with solar illumination, deploy raised floors, and use the building as a thermal mass, are many of the same conclusions we have arrived at in our own work.

If sustainable architecture is take hold, it's important to examine the social responsibilities of the architect. At this point in history, it is an ethical question. In 1987, I was asked by some members of the Jewish Community in New York to conceive a memorial of the Holocaust at Auschwitz-Birkenau. During my visit to the death camp, I realized, on looking at its layout, that designers, architects and engineers actively engaged in the specific questions of how to design a gas chamber for hundreds of people to be executed economically and efficiently. People actually put this project on their drawing boards! The architect, if they recognize the tragedy, ethically has to say, 'I don't do that kind of work.' The question is at what point does an architect engage in social responsibility? At the point when ethical considerations start to become real and manifest in their own decision making. One might say we are still designing gas chambers. If you look at most of the materials made by modern industry and you put them in a sealed glass box with a minimum amount of air in a city with congestion and pollution, you are putting people into gas chambers. Many building materials contain known and serious carcinogens. They have heavy metals, persistent toxins, biochemical substances, and endocrine disrupters. Many of these substances cause genetic mutation, respiratory diseases, cancer and critical birth defects. It's astonishing to think that most of the materials that modern industry makes for our buildings were never designed for indoor use.

What we're now saying is that, instead of designing killing machines, why don't we design living machines? And what's really elegant about Nikken Sekkei's buildings, especially their office designs, for example, is that they're not designing work support systems for people who don't have a life. They're designing life support systems for people who work. Their architectural output is not just about productivity. It's also about human wellbeing made possible by better design. Nikken Sekkei is moving away from a world that is essentially timefully mindless, of its bad effects on nature and the human community, towards a timeless mindfulness in their architecture. They're creating buildings that are comfortable, that are timelessly mindful of the idea of engaging with the natural world and providing you with an awareness of nurture. By contrast, most conventional modern architecture tries to distance itself from such actions, from the human users of buildings and their needs. It has an inclination to neutralize everything.

One of the great challenges of architecture in our time is how should it mirror the flexibility of nature? How can one design something as sophisticated and biologically efficient as...a tree? Nature has a great repository of very elegant design solutions so applicable to advanced building systems. Many of these solutions are the gifts of evolution. It's evident that many of the architects and engineers at Nikken Sekkei are deeply familiar with these powers.

It's important for us to look at the whole continuum of sustainable architecture—it's a long journey. Our initial route has been to attempt to be less destructive by halving the environmental burden. We may think we're designing high tech buildings using ecological principles but, in the end, if these principles are still linked to the same destructive systems that brought us our present afflictions, then what may be required is more than just precautions, codes, reductions and eco-materials. Why not utterly transform design and social systems where we can achieve not just zero environmental dangers but maximize delight and productivity? In our practice in Virginia we try and push the design so that it goes somewhere special. Our credo is 'don't just reduce the load—re-imagine the problem.'

What this portends for the next generation of green architects is the actively solar-powered building. We are starting to see photovoltaic systems that produce electricity so the building becomes like a tree. What we're doing in the building we just designed at Oberlin is very similar to Nikken Sekkei's design for the Tokyo Gas Company's building, Earth Port. Let me say that Earth Port is one of the most well considered green designs I've ever seen. It's an extraordinary amalgam of natural energy strategies and delicate beauty. The Oberlin building also has an atrium, it runs on solar power, purifies its own water in a 'living machine', and it produces more energy than it needs to operate. That's the direction we're going in—designing buildings that make more energy than they need to operate. This will be a major feature of the next industrial revolution. Imagine a building that functions like a tree, that purifies water and makes oxygen. Imagine a building that makes more energy than it ever uses. It would actually pay back its embodied energy mortgage. How about paying back all the energy that was invested in your building? Imagine a world of buildings that were actually productive, not just less destructive.

We're now designing a town for the utility company in northern Indiana where the idea is to design the city like a forest. We're trying to balance economy, equity and ecology, to find a merger of the three institutions where they all can coexist delightfully and profitably. It's a challenge—how do we make a city like a forest? Well, one thing you do is plant a roof, like Nikken Sekkei did in Osaka. It's a meadow now that attracts various local birds flying overhead. The next question is how do we make the roofs of buildings follow photovoltaic systems and absorb solar energy and make electricity?

We're working with utility companies and saying, wouldn't it be interesting if you adopted a product-to-service protocol, and lease the south-facing surfaces of rooftops. And the better oriented it is, the more valuable they will be. And you will put up all the solar collectors, because you know how to make all the utility connections, and you know how to link it into an integrated energy production system. Utility businesses and the telecommunications businesses are ultimately interactive. Information is power. Power is information.

In the future, we may see the electronic era add to what's going on right here on the top of the Earth Port building. This would mean that those surfaces that face south, that are serving the sun, will be producing all the energy for the building. And the utility itself will manage that as a product of service so that the people who occupy the building can go about enjoying life without feeling guilty while the people who are meant to be designing these things are actually engaged in these issues. And that's why what Nikken Sekkei is doing is so important: to signal that intention, to create the platform on which we could then add that next layer or that next dimension, because without the knowledge of their building examples we can't go to the next step. Unless they reduce energy consumption down by 50%, we can't begin to imagine totally powering buildings by the sun. A strong foundation has to be made for this kind of architecture.

An important credo of Nikken Sekkei is 'learning from the old in creating the new'. I think it's a very thoughtful and sensitive stance—a prime example of 'timeless mindfulness'. I believe that what Mr Eiji Maki and his architects are doing is successfully interpreting a traditional design vocabulary into modern terms and doing it with grace, imagination and elegance. In my own practice, 'learning from the old to create the new' might be best expressed in studying how traditional people understood their local climate and local materials, and then you honour the new technology. We have to create the new—we can't slavishly replicate ancient design because historically the materials available were different. And the ancients didn't have the large sheet of glass that we have. However, an important contribution of early architecture is its inherent sustainable qualities: consider the use of straw thatch for roofing—a highly efficient insulator from natural materials, totally bio degradable, and coming with its own earthy aesthetic quality.

We find the influence of Nikken Sekkei's work extremely vital because of the vast range of skills and abilities among their designers and engineers they can command to put at the service of sustainable architecture. It makes them a formidable force in the global promotion of these design principles, which is why this book is so important for western readers and architectural practitioners. This information needs to be out there. We need to know that Japan is a place for this kind of design, and that Nikken Sekkei's extensive body of knowledge is not only accessible, but has proved to be very viable and very successful. They present a really important platform because they allow us to see that we can slow down our destruction. This buys us all time to speculate on moving toward a different trajectory from trying to be less consumptive toward being actually productive. This may be the divergence point for us. We want architecture to transcend the destructive limits that pervade the craft, not just to reduce or halve environmental loads, but to become productive again and create buildings that function as successfully, as organically, as the way trees do. They talk about adaptability and the point that we should not create hybrid materials...a very important idea. And design for dis-assembly is fundamentally critical. They have really hit some of the most important issues of architecture in terms of its material nature—the heterogeneous form, that which is local but unique. Within this form lie the seeds of the building's adaptability—which doesn't mean a return to the homogeneous block building you see in every city in the world.

We believe that if you're going to design a big building in the city, you shouldn't necessarily just design it as an office building with floor plate dimensions that suit the office purpose, but actually design it as housing in the future, and then adapt it to office use. We've done this with many of our projects such as the Nike building, the Gap project and the new headquarters we're designing for IBM in Holland. If you design a living system for people who work, an apartment in which they can work, then you are designing something that has long-term utility.

If we want sustainable ideas to be contagious and fully implemented, then we need everyone concerned at every level of the plan to contribute from the very beginning. We have to insist on having the engineer and the landscape architect in the room from the first day. These forces and talents are part of the design. They're not inseparable. That bright green roof on the Osaka Gymnasium is the design. We actually bring in all the people that are going to build and use the project at the same time to discuss the goals of the design. Similar to Nikken Sekkei, we find integrated design teams absolutely critical to many aspects of this work. What's delightful about it is that you can engage everyone's skills and passion for the work. This is the new design protocol, and it does involve all of us.

From certain architectural attitudes in the not-so-distant past here in the west, it seems that some designers viewed users of buildings as invisible. Take, for example, 'sick' buildings—environments that make people physically ill, very possibly because the end user and their wellbeing weren't configured into the design. I believe that Nikken Sekkei is very aware of the end user as a key element in the planning process. Respect for the user is expressed in many of Nikken Sekkei's designs through the classical Japanese concept of Ireko, which embraces a whole structural vocabulary to do with the dynamics of spatial flow between the interior and the outside world. This idea of spatial zoning in a dwelling or an office space where you find a completely sympathetic relationship between the interstices of a building and the ambient and personal zones is a fundamental element of traditional Japanese architecture that is so elegant. It lends a certain poetic element to both the Japanese house and office design and considers the user by allowing them autonomy and choice in the personal zone and community with others in the ambient zone. This spatial poetry is a gift from their designers to us, and it's so evident in buildings like the Institute for Advanced Studies and the Lake Biwa Museum complex.

The idea of using traditional techniques and practised concepts is magnificent. I notice that many of Nikken Sekkei's buildings have eaves, only now they're made of glass. I'm glad these elements are still there. They still work, so why throw them away? These are fundamental, timeless values that we can reuse, and it's great that they're transforming these features into modern forms. I like the fact that they have words for these features, such as 'engawa' and 'sudare', which connect the design process to culture.

As I mentioned earlier, I think Nikken Sekkei represents a brilliant synthesis and a hugely successful platform for the future of design integration. Please note the importance of that word 'future'. We've established that sustainable design has a continuum and that within this continuum there are various practitioners all over the world looking for the same destination but performing their work on different trajectories. Certain architectural conventions are not revolutionized overnight—there is no instant miracle that will give us clean air in a split second. We are in a constant state of 'becoming'; it's an evolutionary pattern and we must be patient with the learning process, with the unfolding. If you look at the enormous range of innovations Nikken Sekkei and William McDonough & Partners have achieved in sustainable design from different sides of the world, you'll find that we've all come a long way from our starting points. This, in itself, is a foundation for great hope, for great change.

When we define the progress of sustainable design as a series of constantly-evolving transformations, we need to examine what strategies we're using to effect those changes. In our case, and I'm sure this is true for Nikken Sekkei, rather than separating ourselves from the realities of the industrial world, always regarded as a malignant source of environmental ills, we find it more creative to engage with it and seed the ground for transformation. It's a process, I believe, that Nikken Sekkei is very good at, functioning as they do in an extraordinarily aggressive industrial nation. One can say today that sustainable design is a revolutionary architectural movement that challenges established institutions created by commerce and technology.

Most firms engaging in ecologically considered architecture adopt the approach of using less energy and resources over time. But that still comes down to the idea of being less bad. It slows the problem of environmental damage but doesn't necessarily eliminate it. What we're trying to do in our practice is sequester materials into biological and/or technical cycles and not create monstrous hybrids. This means trying to design buildings for disassembly, whereby they're either designed for the biological nutrient system or the technical nutrient system. Steel to steel, glass to glass. This means building with materials designed to return to the world's fundamental metabolisms—either a biological or an industrial metabolism. It's a basic principle of waste equals food, where everything is a nutrient for something else, just as in nature. Things come from nature and return to nature. We do not see nature as necessarily efficient, we see it as effective and celebrate its abundance. We call this eco-effective design rather than eco-efficient. This concept asks us to delight in the cherry tree in the spring with all its exuberance—certainly it is not efficient with a thousand short-lived blossoms, but what a joy to behold its gesture of promise, beauty and hope.

In the same way we must, with deep respect, delight in the hopeful creativity and the impact of Nikken Sekkei's architecture, which has yet to be fully realized by the world architecture community. Here is one of the most important design firms in the world, which understands the language of commerce, is thoughtful and innovative, and holds a place of great influence in the continuum of ecologically intelligent design. This work is the soil, to coin an appropriate metaphor, in which young architects will plant the seeds of the next generation of sustainable architecture in Japan.

RITE Head Office building, Kyoto. Innovative bulding technology in harmony with the surrounding landscape.

Katashi Matsunawa
Director,
Nikken Sekkei, Tokyo

The Nikken Sekkei
Approach to
Green Buildings

Nikken Sekkei has been designing and constructing buildings for a hundred years. This longevity as architects has allowed us to accumulate a deep knowledge of our art, which, in turn, has stimulated and maintained our pace with developing technologies, new building materials and evolving social forces. Through many decades we have seen the urban landscape change rapidly as Japan has grown to become an intensely industrialized nation. Such growth has not been without its price with respect to architecture and its impact on the environment. We believe that a profound change is needed in the way buildings are designed and in the way they function. In common with many designers around the world, we at Nikken Sekkei have been working towards a vision of 'green buildings', an increasingly important concept that will influence forever the way architects think about buildings, their material nature and how their design benefits the human community. We hope that our ideas, as presented in this book, will make a valuable contribution to the continuing learning process of how to produce a sustainable architecture so that it becomes a vital part of a sustainable future. We have set ourselves three goals for the creation of our green buildings: they must create attractive spaces, they must draw on the benefits of nature, and their environmental impact must be half that of recent buildings designed by conventional standards (figure 1). These three goals are synergistic; success in one enhances the others and the greatest benefit comes when all three are attained through the entire lifecycle of the building, from design through construction, operation, renovation and disposal.

For example, attractive buildings are popular and stay in service longer, and an extended service life reduces impact on the environment. When the natural environment is allowed to exert beneficial effects on the building, it becomes more attractive and also requires less energy to function. Longer life, reduced energy consumption and the use of environment-friendly materials ('eco-materials') are the key guidelines for reducing environmental impact. A building that creates an attractive, natural environment will have happier, healthier and more productive occupants. It will enhance the environment outside as well as inside, creating charming streets and pleasing skylines.

The owners and users of green buildings are not just 'doing the right thing'. This is true for both dwellings and commercial projects. If the building is designed well, they will see benefits on the bottom line in the form of reduced absenteeism, higher productivity, higher rental value and smaller bills. Thus, green buildings are practical as well as attractive and they provide broader benefits than reduced environmental impact.

Buildings and the Environment – Why Green Architecture is Necessary

The mass production and consumption of goods in the 20th century drains the earth's resources and generates enormous volumes of waste, polluting the air, water and soil and spawning global environmental threats. Among them, the global warming problem is particularly ominous and raises worldwide concern. The predicted rise in sea levels produced by accelerated global warming and its effects on human life and ecological systems will be immense and threatens catastrophe for many of the world's coastlines [1] (figure 2). Over the course of the 20th century the consumption of fossil energy rose 17-fold worldwide and 74-fold in Japan (figures 3a and 3b). Carbon dioxide released into the atmosphere by the profligate burning of fossil fuels is the dominant factor behind global warming (figure 4). The continuing growth of energy consumption, particularly in Asia, is predicted to lead to an explosive growth in CO_2 emissions (figures 5a, 5b, 6, 7a and 7b).

Our future demands the immediate reduction of the use of fossil energy and the burden it places on the planet. However, as consumption in developing countries booms and those nations fail to exercise controls, or live within current high levels, we are far from even restraining its growth. Figure 8 plots the levels of environmental impact produced by various annual rates of impact reduction. If the annual rate is 1%, it will take 70 years to reduce the impact by half. Contrary to the assumption employed here, the number of CO_2-producing facilities is increasing continuously and the world is very far from achieving a 1% reduction rate. [2] Reduction of environmental damage requires technological innovation and drastic socioeconomic changes.

Why Designers are Required to Find Answers

The uniquely characteristic architectural forms of each region and nation, which have evolved in response to the local climate and character, are being

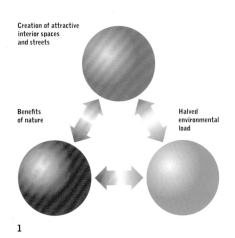

Creation of attractive
interior spaces
and streets

Benefits
of nature

Halved
environmental
load

1

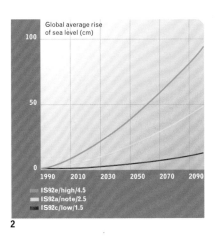

Global average rise
of sea level (cm)

100

50

0

1990   2010   2030   2050   2070   2090

IS92e/high/4.5
IS92a/note/2.5
IS92c/low/1.5

2

21

1 The three key elements of
green buildings.
2 Predicted rise of sea levels
(Source: second IPCC report).

3a Movements in worldwide
consumption of fossil energy.
3b Movements in
consumption of fossil energy
in Japan (1880–1995;
Industrial Culture Research).
4 Average CO$_2$ concentration
at the Mauna Loa Observatory
in Hawaii.

5a Forecast for worldwide
primary energy consumption.
5b Forecast for Asian primary
energy consumption.
6 Movement of worldwide CO$_2$
generation.

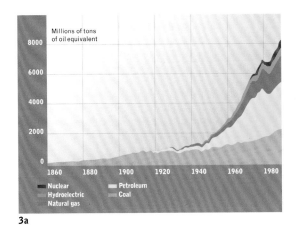

3a

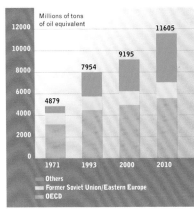

5a

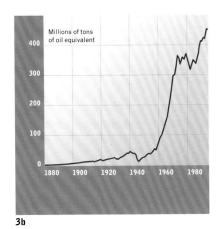

3b

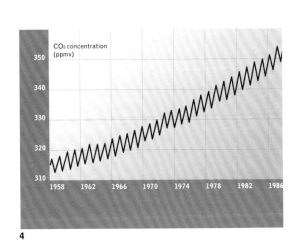

4

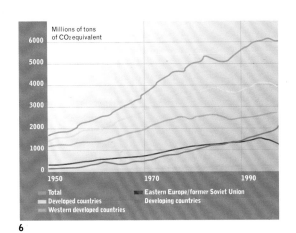

6

7a Breakdown of worldwide
CO$_2$ emissions (1994).
7b Per capita CO$_2$ generation
(1994).

8 Scenario for halving
environmental impact
(environmental load reduction
rate and changes over time).

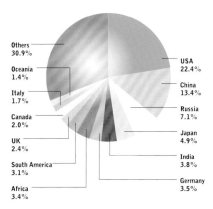

7a

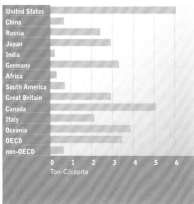

7b

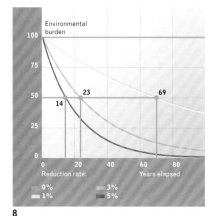

8

supplanted by uniform building designs predicated on the mass consumption of fossil fuels. Apart from the destruction that affects regional cultures on many levels, this approach is extraordinarily wasteful. A rough calculation of CO$_2$ generation in Japan (figure 9) indicates that 36% of Japan's CO$_2$ emissions are due to buildings, largely in the form of energy consumption. The three main types of energy consumption in buildings are air conditioning, lighting and conveyance, the movement of people, objects, air and water (figure 14). Buildings that generate a smaller environmental detriment are a key element in reducing total environmental impact. All those who create, own and maintain buildings have a great responsibility in this regard.

Can We Halve the Environmental Impact of Buildings?

Before we answer this question, we need some yardstick to quantify environmental impact. The most widely used indicator is Life Cycle CO$_2$ (LCCO$_2$). CO$_2$ is the major cause of global warming. LCCO$_2$ measures the environmental impact of a building over all the stages of its life, from the design through its demolition and disposal, in terms of the equivalent volume of CO$_2$ emission. Figure 10 illustrates an example of a calculation for the LCCO$_2$ of a Japanese office building. The top bar of figure 10 proves that the largest element in the building's LCCO$_2$ is the energy consumed in its operation. The environmental effects of construction and demolition are also substantial. Therefore the most important elements in LCCO$_2$ reduction are, in order:
1. energy saving
2. extending the life of the building
3. use of eco-materials.

The other three bars of figure 10 show the approximate LCCO$_2$ reduction per year that these three measures could yield. Halving the energy used in running the building would reduce LCCO$_2$ by approximately 30%. Extending the life of a building from 35 years to 100 years raises the LCCO$_2$ reduction to approximately 40%. The use of recycled materials such as blast-furnace cement could bring the LCCO$_2$ reduction to as much as 50%. Thus, there is a realistic prospect of reducing environmental impact by half.

Learning from Traditional Buildings

Traditional Japanese buildings offer superb examples of what we are trying to achieve in our buildings for the new century and the future. Their underlying principle is amity with the environment. They are close to nature and tailored to local conditions in ways that provide comfort with minimal energy consumption. Indigenous buildings in Japan that existed before the age of mass fossil energy consumption successfully minimized the environmental load, and were filled with elegant techniques for making use of natural energy. Such architecture avoids artificial uniformity, creating instead attractive and heterogeneous interior spaces and harmonious spatial relationships. These structures were designed to last and were built from renewable, locally available materials. We aim to learn the lessons offered by these superbly functional traditional buildings and apply them in our own green designs.

Buildings that exist harmoniously with nature have expression and forms that reflect the local land and climate. They also create delightful streets and towns. Traditional buildings are designed to arrive at a comfortable environmental balance through passive techniques. But the perception of comfort conditions in traditional buildings differs from modern perceptions. There was no intention of setting constant, arbitrary conditions of temperature and humidity. Neither was there any attempt to produce a constant, uniform lighting level. In traditional buildings, comfort was sought within acceptable ranges, with consideration being given to a comprehensive comfort including visual and aural aspects.

Component Technologies

The design principle embodied in traditional buildings, that they should regulate themselves to reach a comfortable environment without assistance, can be applied to the component technologies of a wide range of buildings.

Deep eaves or verandahs to block the sun's rays

The first step towards creating buildings that use natural energy is to prevent heat entering and to block sunlight. Japanese traditional buildings tend

9 The composition of Japan's environmental impact (the building-related share in Japan's CO$_2$ emissions in 1990).

10 Calculation of LCCO$_2$ for an office building.
11 Movements in the composition of Japan's energy consumption (industrial/commercial/transportation).

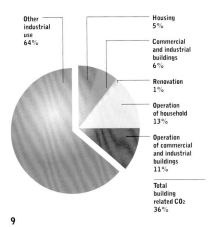

Other industrial use 64%

Housing 5%

Commercial and industrial buildings 6%

Renovation 1%

Operation of household 13%

Operation of commercial and industrial buildings 11%

Total building related CO$_2$ 36%

9

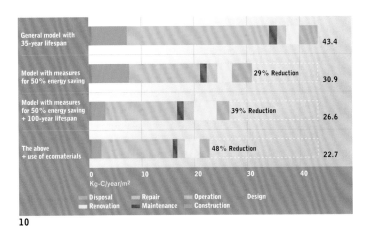

General model with 35-year lifespan — 43.4

Model with measures for 50% energy saving — 29% Reduction — 30.9

Model with measures for 50% energy saving + 100-year lifespan — 39% Reduction — 26.6

The above + use of ecomaterials — 48% Reduction — 22.7

Kg-C/year/m^2 — 0 10 20 30 40

Disposal | Repair | Operation | Design
Renovation | Maintenance | Construction

10

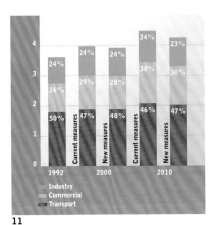

1992 | 2000 | 2010

Industry
Commercial
Transport

11

to emphasize sunlight blocking, while allowing air to pass through the structure. The main methods used are deep eaves to keep direct sunlight out of the rooms in summer, supplemented by shitomi (latticed shutters) and sudare (rattan blinds) (photos 15, 16, 17). Deciduous trees planted near houses only block sunlight in summer, when they have leaves. Besides using natural energy, these methods lend character and aesthetic features to buildings (photo 18).

Shoji screens for pleasant lighting

Shoji screens are a traditional way of drawing light in and dispersing it throughout a room. The appearance of the screens varies with changing patterns of daylight and shadow, creating a sense of connection between interior and exterior (photos 19, 20) .

Uchimizu (sprayed water) to use the transpiration effect

Water sprayed on paths, courtyards and elsewhere makes use of the water's latent heat of evaporation to lower the air temperature (photo 21).

Engawa (wood-floored verandah)

The engawa or verandah space is interposed as a buffer between the outside and the 'zashiki' rooms (living rooms with tatami mat floors). Daylight passing through the shoji screens is dispersed throughout the rooms within. In fine weather the shoji and other barriers can be thrown open to let the breeze from outside flow into the living space, or closed to varying degrees to regulate the flow of cold outside air to the living rooms. The engawa is a space for drawing in and using natural energy, while blocking unwanted light and heat. It is also a place to sit quietly and enjoy the natural environment outside (photo 22).

Flexible use of space

The inner rooms of traditional Japanese houses are separated by shoji screens or fusuma (sliding doors) rather than by fixed walls. This construction allows the available space to be partitioned into smaller rooms or merged into larger spaces as required by the occupants and their activities.

The flexible use of space is traditional in Japanese architecture (photos 23 and 24). By removing the shoji screen in summer, we can enjoy an open-air atmosphere. When the shoji screen is in place, we can appreciate the soft sunlight it provides.

The Ireko Concept of Spatial Zoning

In traditional buildings, the elements described above are combined in a spatial composition that enhances their effects and forms a balanced environment that is both comfortable and aesthetically close to nature. Space in Japanese traditional houses is not simply divided between interior and exterior. Instead, a variety of spaces exist in the interstices, creating a pleasantly heterogeneous environment that has real depth while remaining close to nature. The basis of the Ireko concept is the spatial flow from outdoor space through to semi-outdoor space, semi-indoor space, indoor space and local indoor spaces. We aim to take the traditional Ireko concept of space as our model, to redefine it from a new viewpoint, and put that concept into effect in spaces that harness the benefits of nature to minimize the environmental load (figure 12).

Outdoor spaces

The landscape and greenery outside a traditional building serve to moderate the harsher outside environment and are essential for the formation of a pleasant, self-balancing indoor space. On a broader environmental level, the area of paved ground is reduced, limiting the heat island effect and absorbing rain to replenish groundwater. The foliage preserves privacy by blocking lines of sight, baffles noise and absorbs CO$_2$. Natural topography and original flora should be retained to avoid standardized uniformity in the landscaping design (photos 25, 26).

Intermediate spaces

The intermediate spaces that exist between indoors and outdoors are particularly important for defining the relationship between the two. Within the Ireko spatial hierarchy they can be divided between the semi-outdoor and the semi-indoor areas.

12 The hierarchy of Ireko
space.
13 The load must be halted at
the source.
14 Configuration of energy
consumption in the operation
of an office building.

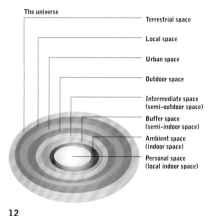

The universe

Terrestrial space

Local space

Urban space

Outdoor space

Intermediate space
(semi-outdoor space)

Buffer space
(semi-indoor space)

Ambient space
(indoor space)

Personal space
(local indoor space)

12

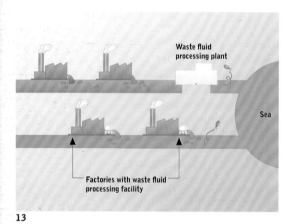

Waste fluid
processing plant

Sea

Factories with waste fluid
processing facility

13

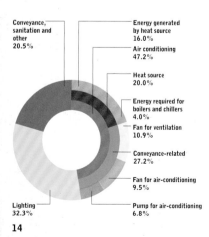

Conveyance,
sanitation and
other
20.5%

Energy generated
by heat source
16.0%

Air conditioning
47.2%

Heat source
20.0%

Energy required for
boilers and chillers
4.0%

Fan for ventilation
10.9%

Conveyance-related
27.2%

Fan for air-conditioning
9.5%

Lighting
32.3%

Pump for air-conditioning
6.8%

14

Rodai (balconies or decks) are the main type of semi-outdoor space. They are not completely outdoors, but they're very close. They have some protection from the sun, but their temperature will always be very close to outdoors.

The engawa is the main example of a semi-indoor space. Likewise, this is not totally indoors, but close. This kind of space closely reflects outdoor variations in light, wind and air temperature. These spaces draw natural energy into the interior while allowing the occupants to experience the natural environment outside. Other examples of intermediate space are the atrium, the conservatories seen in certain northern nations and the balconies found on buildings in many southern countries.

Drawing nature into the interior is not always a good thing. With their apertures screened or closed, intermediate spaces can serve as valuable insulative buffer zones against glaring sunshine or chill winds. Outer corridors and perimeter aisles are also effective buffer spaces (photo 22, 27).

Indoor spaces

The idea of consuming fossil energy for lighting and air conditioning to maintain a constant, uniform indoor environment has been a dominant theme in modern building design for decades. If this approach is abandoned in favour of the formation of a heterogeneous indoor environment, the inhabited areas can be divided into ambient zones and personal zones. In the former, a considerable variation in conditions such as temperature and brightness is acceptable, and the indoor spaces enjoy more buffering from the outside. Therefore the zero energy band can be expanded in the ambient areas, thus using more natural energy in place of fossil energy. In traditional Japanese buildings, this space is analogous to the zashiki, the living rooms floored with tatami matting. Within ambient zones there are local, personal zones. Such planning is the essence of the Ireko concept. In a traditional Japanese house the main local space was around the hibachi, a small charcoal brazier. Heating the whole zashiki to a uniform temperature was impossible, so people would gather around the hibachi for warmth in this personal, local environment. In a modern office building, the workstation booth is a personal environment that can be equipped with task lighting and personal air conditioning, allowing individuals to produce an environment as close as possible to their personal preferences (photo 28).

A Comprehensive Approach to Energy-Saving Buildings

Consideration of the methods described below must begin from the earliest stages of the design process. The orientation of the building and its position on the site has a strong influence on how and when sunlight and air currents can enter, thus affecting daylight, air conditioning, ventilation and many other aspects. The efficacy of passive methods included at later design stages depends to a large extent on the initial decision on how to situate the building within its immediate habitat.

Cutting off loads at the source

It is important to cut off environmental loads at their point of origin (figure 13). It is easier to remove waste at the source, in the factory, than to remove it later by treating the entire river. Similarly, it is easier to capture waste heat near an indoor source, or to block its entry from an outdoor source, than to allow it to mix and then work to cool the entire air mass. This principle applies more broadly to the handling of building materials, which we will discuss later. The first step that should be taken to reduce energy consumption for air conditioning and lighting is halting the loads at source by blocking direct sunlight, improving insulation and other means. The use of highly insulative materials in structures that block the flow of heat into the interior space is an effective approach. Double glazing and double-glazed insulative sashes are effective for windows.

In assessing how energy consumption is configured in a building's operation, heat, conveyance and lighting require the highest percentages (figure 14). Blinds or eaves can be used to block direct sunlight and, if possible, planting a lawn and trees around the building will stop both direct and reflected sunlight. The form and location of the building itself are also significant. Facing the windows north and south and blocking the sun from the west reduces the cooling load considerably. Personal computers and other office equipment generate heat that increases the air temperature. Therefore, it's essential to capture waste heat from these sources and have it absorbed locally. This prevents it from mixing with the rest of the air in the room.

15 Deep eaves to keep direct
sunlight out of the rooms in
summer.
16 Shitomi, latticed shutters.

15

16

19 Shoji screens, located at
north and south, draw sunlight into the room.
20 The shadows of branches
swinging in the wind fall on
the shoji.

19

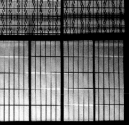

21 Water sprayed on paths.
22 Engawa, wood-floored
verandah.

21

22

When the shoji screen is in
place, we can appreciate the
soft sunlight it provides.

23

24

25 The air moving across the
pool produce cool breezes
inside the building.
26 The ground surface around
the building is covered with
soil and plants.

25

26

31

27 Rodai, balconies.
28 The local indoor space
(hibachi).

27

28

Use of Natural Energy

Passive methods should be used first, in order to gain the full benefits of natural energy. Where natural energy falls short, active methods such as artificial heating and lighting can be implemented as supplementary energy.

Daylight use

Ideally, a building using daylight should not be very deep. If it's designed to be deep, it should be able to take in light on two sides. Natural lighting requires light paths that will carry the light to the heart of the building. Elements such as light shelves, top lights and light ducts are effective for carrying light into building interiors.

Natural ventilation

Natural air movement in a building feels pleasant and can greatly reduce the energy consumed for air conditioning. Natural air movement requires the formation of air paths, which can be enhanced by orienting the building to the prevailing wind and regulated using user-adjustable apertures. Gravity ventilation provides natural airflow in the absence of wind by making use of the difference in density between indoor and outdoor air. The wind tower is another way of enhancing natural ventilation. Wind speed is generally higher at the top of the wind tower, creating a pressure differential that moves air. Gravity ventilation is also enhanced. In some situations an atrium can also function as a wind tower.

Storage masses

Natural energy can be banked in storage masses (massive sections of the building) and later retrieved, as required. The most common example is night cooling by outside air, in which cold night air is drawn into the building to cool its mass. The stored cold mass is then utilized to cool the building's interior during the day. This is a particularly effective method in intelligent buildings that require cooling all year round.

Power generation from natural energy

Natural energy from the wind and sun can be used to generate electricity for sale or for building use and also the solar energy utilized directly for heating.

Water usage

Japan has abundant rainwater (around 1500mm per year) which can be collected and used as greywater of all kinds, thus saving valuable water resources. Wastewater can be used for toilet flushing or plant watering after preliminary treatment. Rainwater and pre-treated wastewater should be directed to a permeable ground surface to replenish urban groundwater. Residual pollutants in the pre-treated wastewater will be biodegraded in the soil without further treatment, providing nutrients for plants.

Rooftop planting

The rooftop of a building receives the most exposure to the sun, so insulation there is particularly important. Covering the roof with soil and growing plants on it is one way of improving insulation. The evaporation of water from the soil and the plants removes latent heat of evaporation from the roof, cooling the building below.

Making effective use of energy

In order to save energy, it is important to use all energy effectively. Those responsible for equipment and system selection must be prepared to choose, and pay for, high-efficiency equipment options and adopt energy-saving systems such as total energy systems and heat-recovery systems. Co-generation systems are a leading type of total energy system, while heat-storage heat pumps are a leading type of heat recovery system.

Exploitation of unused energy

It is important to recover the unused waste energy and exploit it as a substitute for fossil energy. For example, heat from river and wastewater can be used by utilizing heatpumps and heat exchangers.

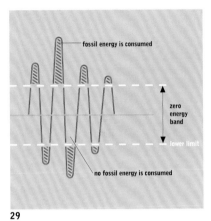

29

Precise operation and control

Sloppy control and operation practices invite enormous energy losses, which must be avoided. Cooperative control is essential for the effective integration of passive and active methods. Effective use of daylight requires a cooperative lighting control system to ensure that artificial lights are turned off when the level of daylight permits. Ventilation control systems can now control window opening for optimum ventilation.

Enhanced energy management

Systems for energy management in buildings, such as Building and Energy Management Systems (BEMS), must be developed to keep managers informed of how much energy is being used and where in a building. Ideally, it should be possible to compare energy usage against a planned energy budget. Fault Detection and Diagnosis (FDD) systems are now being developed to detect and diagnose operational faults, which can cause major increases in environmental loads. The next stage is Building Optimization, Fault Detection and Diagnosis (BOFDD), which includes the optimization of building operation.

Electricity generation and load levelling

Any surplus electrical energy produced in the building by photovoltaic, wind or co-generation can be stored for later use, but in some countries where it is legally possible, such as Japan, the surplus may be sold to power companies. This makes economic sense for the building owner, it also makes generation equipment a more attractive purchase, and helps power companies with load levelling which can avoid the need for power station construction.

Making Maximum Use of the Zero Energy Band

The range in which neither heating nor cooling are required is called the 'zero energy band', because no energy is consumed at all. Heating or cooling only becomes necessary when the room temperature starts to move beyond this temperature range. The same principle applies to lighting and ventilation. Indoor conditions can be maintained within these bands for a considerable portion of the year without consuming energy (figure 29). Insulation, sun screening and natural energy can be used to extend the use of the zero energy band for as long as possible. When daylight provides adequate lighting, the air is fresh enough, and the temperature is comfortable, no further energy expenditure is required. However, occupants and managers must find and establish the most suitable zero energy bands and avoid needless energy consumption within the band.

The width of the zero energy band is never uniform. In a room with a high ceiling it is quite adequate to maintain good conditions in an inhabited zone up to a height of around 1.8m from the floor, without trying to do so in the entire volume of the room. A wider zero energy band can be employed in unoccupied and ambient spaces than in occupied and personal spaces.

Creating Heterogeneous Spaces

Spaces don't need to be maintained in a uniform, homogeneous state and it is wasteful to do so. Lighting and air conditioning needs in a space vary from place to place and over time. Such needs can be met locally and by flexible processes. Thus the broadest possible zero energy band can be utilized in each area without sacrificing comfort where it is needed. The heterogeneous spaces that result consume less energy and are more interesting and attractive.

Extending the Life of Buildings

For a building to have a long life, it must be well maintained, satisfying to its users, and able to cope with the demands of progress, such as computerization. Personal computers require power supply and communication cable access, and the heat they generate necessitates larger HVAC systems. It may be impossible to fit these into an old building. The flexibility to expand or replace any equipment is an important element in designing for building longevity.

This kind of flexibility is ensured by generous floor-to-floor heights, double floors and equipment space above the false ceiling and on the roof and balconies. Ample vertical space for routing building services must also be made available. Durable equipment with ample upgrade options should be selected, but it will still be replaced more often than the building. Replacement space must be available so that equipment can be in use continually up to the point of its replacement and carried out of the building with minimum disruption.

Materials must be chosen for durability and ease of maintenance so that they will remain attractive and sound over a long life span.

Appropriate Use of Materials

Materials are an important consideration for green buildings throughout their lifecycle. Optimum material choices must be made with consideration of the construction, use and eventual disposal of the building. The use of materials such as natural wood and stone, in place of those that consume large amounts of energy in their manufacture, is effective in reducing the environmental impact. If the use of non-natural materials is unavoidable, it must be conditional on other advantages, such as a longer life span or reduced maintenance, which compensate for the additional $LCCO_2$ cost.

Locally produced natural materials should be used wherever possible to avoid using excessive energy in their transportation. The principle of 'no mixing' can be applied broadly to the choice and use of buildings. If the materials from a demolished building can be properly divided and collected separately, it becomes possible to recycle them. When separation of materials starts at the design stage, the potential for recycling buildings is enhanced. The design should provide for easy disassembly rather than destructive demolition wherever possible. Composite materials should be avoided because they cannot be re-separated efficiently after use.

Recycled materials should be used to reduce the use of new materials. As well as reused building materials, recycled materials include steel mill by-products such as blast furnace cement and 'electrosteel' reinforcement recycled from scrap steel.

Not all materials consumed in construction form parts of the building. Packaging and form-work are often discarded from construction sites in enormous quantities. The selection of materials and construction methods must take into account the secondary wastes that will be generated. Designers should take the lead in promoting responsible packaging of materials and reuse of materials such as form-work.

It is inevitable that some waste will be generated, but the designer must consider what the wastes will be. Hazardous or environmentally harmful substances must be collected and disposed of according to international rules to render them harmless. This is possible, but costly, and the designer can't guarantee that harmful wastes will be handled properly after a building life span of a hundred years. Therefore, it's better to cut off such disposal problems at the source by avoiding materials that could generate harmful waste.

Notes
1. The IPCC, an international organization of scientists and experts working to evaluate the impact of global warming, has predicted that unless human activity changes it will lead to accelerated global warming and sea levels rising by tens of centimetres and perhaps a metre over the next few decades.

2. This is a guideline calculation which, for the sake of simplicity, makes the optimistic assumption that no new CO_2-producing facilities are built.

Kakegawa City Hall, Shizuoka
Prefecture. Fusion between
the human community, nature
and architecture in a civic
space.

Ten Green Buildings by
Nikken Sekkei

International
Institute for
Advanced Studies

Location:
Kyoto

Site area:
40,166 m²

Building area:
5,251 m²

Total floor area:
6,039 m²

Building purpose:
Research centre

Number of floors:
+2

Structure:
RC, S

Completed:
1993

1.1 The view from the patio
of the Community Hall of the
pond and research block.

The Grand Shoin Reinterpreted

The International Institute for Advanced
Studies is Japan's first independent facility
committed to futuristic research on a wide
range of subjects. With participation of
renowned scholars from around the world,
intellectual inquiry at the Institute has ranged
from a comparative study of happiness to
molecular systematics. As a setting for high-
level scientific dialogue and investigation,
the built environment here is imbued with a
pervasive tranquillity. Indeed, the calm,
monastic atmosphere is among the many
deliberate elements resulting from the
Institute's design. Nikken Sekkei approached
the project as a respectful distillation of a
pure, Japanese classical style that balances

function and nature with the meditative
space. Utilizing both modern and traditional
materials and passive technologies, the
buildings and gardens of the IIAS pay
unaffected homage to traditional architecture
from Kyoto and the surrounding district.

The Architectural Continuum and its Influences

IIAS is situated in an area of Kyoto
Prefecture that is abundant with Japanese
architectural history. The city flourished
as the seat of the Japanese imperial court
for over a thousand years, resulting in some
of the finest architecture to be found in the
Asiatic world. In 1994, UNESCO designated
17 regional buildings as World Cultural
Heritage sites. A dominant thread running

through these architectural expressions is
the structure's harmonious relationship to its
environment. Nature and its calming
presence was adopted as a vital constituent
of design evident in the highly-mannered
asceticism of houses, temples and gardens.
Buildings from these periods defined living
spaces freely through the use of open-
planned rooms, cypress bark roofs, wooden
columns, wide, tiered verandahs, folding
screens, tatami matting and deep eaves.
Such temples and shrines are the reserves of
many ancient building traditions and it's easy
to see how the design of IIAS falls within the
architectural continuum.

The arrival of Buddhism in Japan had
a lasting impact on the nation's architecture.

In the periods that followed, the country moved away from outside influences to evolve a purely indigenous Japanese style shaped by the emergence of Zen, the Samurai culture, and the Shogunate. Buddhism resulted in many teaching institutions being built throughout Japan where education and research were a sacred responsibility and Zen monasteries became sites of a constantly shifting guest population. Visiting priests, monks and novices alike were required to contribute their wisdom to the prevailing body of knowledge during their residency. The Toguido Hall of the Jishoji Temple (the Silver Pavilion) (1333–1573), is one of the finest expressions of the relationship between architecture and religion. It is the

first built example of the 'shoin-zukuri' or 'grand shoin' form, a perfected style that would become the precursor of modern Japanese residential architecture. The primary word 'shoin' is translated as 'study hall', a place of learning and meditation.

Architecture as a Haven for the Mind
The 'shoin' of IIAS has been called 'a forum for agreeable contemplation and exchange'. It is a residential/research complex named the 'Scholar's Village' where visiting professors conduct research and share their findings in an open and totally supportive atmosphere. The Institute also has quiet, private spaces for reading, writing and just thinking.

The building site lies in a forested basin among the rolling hills of Keihanna, an area known for brilliant sunny days disrupted by high humidity, heavy rains and sudden mists. However, the consistent moisture factor endows the landscape with dazzling swathes of green, and causes a riotous blooming of cedar, cypress, cherry and ginko trees plus abundant flora indigenous to the area. (This weather pattern has long supported the flourishing of good timber for building materials in this region.)

The IIAS complex is generously positioned on the site using the traditional Ganko design, which produces a tiered or staggered construction. This form was chosen as a coping strategy against the

1.2 Site plan.
1.3 The Keihanna hills
shrouded in mist.
1.4 Western view of the
Institute.

1.5 The south façade showing
the research facilities in a
traditional Ganko (tier)
arrangement with a reflecting
pond. The plan evokes a quiet
and open environment.
1.6 East view of the garden
and part of the residential
wing with balconies.

1.3

1.4

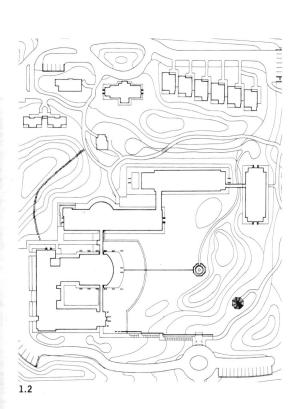

1.2

inconsistent weather and to facilitate
easy contact among staff and researchers.
The site plan establishes the principal
building, with its deeply pitched roof, to the
west with adjacent structures running
on a long plane in a stepped sequence left of
the central body. The main entrance is
accessed via a circular drive. All the
buildings are low two-floor structures with
verandahs running the length of both
façades. Wide eaves shield the balcony level,
allowing the space to be used for human
interaction and transit. The verandah space
is reminiscent of early Japanese temple
porches and serves to keep the interior cool
and dry while allowing access to the
exterior.

The landscaping scheme at the
IIAS was designed to unify the exterior space
between the building block and the surrounding terrain. Classically laid-out gardens
providing serene vistas for the residents
are displayed throughout the property.
Banks of trees and flowering shrubs partially
separate certain areas to create intimate,
secluded groves and walkways. Man-made
ponds and rivulets are strategically located as
part of the consciously-planned scenery.
The ponds are constructed and positioned
for their reflective qualities. The entire
exterior surroundings are a successful
orchestration designed to engender an aura
of quietude and contemplation.

Bringing Nature Indoors

The interior design of the complex was
conceived to maintain an aesthetic continuity
with the natural environment visible beyond
the windows. The buildings comprise a
community hall, a seminar lounge, administration offices, laboratories, a library, and
a lecture theatre. Each of the research
laboratories provides a comfortable haven
that allows for both work and relaxation.
These rooms are basic but not austere and
are equipped with desk units, sofas and
spacious windows that permit gentle breezes
to enter. The interior lighting is also muted
and recessed above the seating and study
areas. All of the labs open onto the gardens,
permitting the residents to leave their desks

1.5

1.6

to meet each other or to seek solitude for their thoughts.

The community hall in the main building functions as an informal communication space for guests and visitors. Its windows extend from the floor to the ceiling of the second level, allowing the entry of natural light for most of the day. The entrance has a curved frontage that opens on to an outdoor lounge with a spacious patio set before a still, reflecting pond.

The seminar lounge of the research block has windows that are open to the garden on two sides, allowing for cross ventilation. Light-filtering screens shelter the expansive window units and smaller panes above them give a tranquil symmetry to the walls. The space is configured to adapt to academic debates, tutorial discussions and social gatherings.

Natural Ventilation Strategies to Combat Humidity

The periods of high humidity were a particular challenge to the Nikken Sekkei design team. It was essential that the living quarters provide visiting scholars with an agreeable temperature zone while utilizing natural air movement to aerate the buildings without having to resort to any artificial intervention or mechanical airflow systems. This dictated the use of large tiled roofs with deep eaves and wide window openings. Ensuring a cross breeze was essential; it is facilitated by the verandahs extending down either side of the dwelling units. The balcony on the second level is designed to cool the hot air near the windows. It too has the effect of encouraging through-breezes. Covered connecting through-ways between buildings are another defence against the heat, humidity and rain.

The architectural innovations incorporated into the design, that in ancient practice collaborated with the natural world to create buildings of harmony and grace, are proven at this site to still be as adaptable, durable and as enhancing to the environment as they were a thousand years ago.

IIAS has hosted many renowned international meetings on several diverse subjects. In 1994, they presented an important

1.7 Strategically-placed
eaves direct diffuse sunlight
into the seminar lounge.
1.8 A study and residential
office. Each room opens on to
the garden. Windows are
equipped with light screens
and are designed to permit
natural ventilation.

1.9 The seminar lounge of
the research block with a view
of the garden. The windows
and lighting design are derived
from traditional Japanese
interiors. The space can be
used for meetings, seminars
and social functions.

1.8

1.7

workshop devoted to the 'Structure of the
Intercultural World' that focused on how
each culture directly enters into another and
is made richer by the presence and
integration of the unknown element. It seems
appropriate that such a subject should be
studied in a building whose design so
eloquently expresses the synthesis of many
classical influences fused with contemporary
sustainable architecture.
(Architect: Hisashi Yosano)

1.10 Sketch of the eaves as
sunlight deflectors.
1.11 and 1.12 Drawings of
the Ganko scheme.
1.13 The research block
elevation and section.
1.14 View of the office area.

1.10

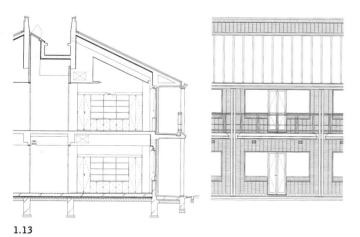

1.13

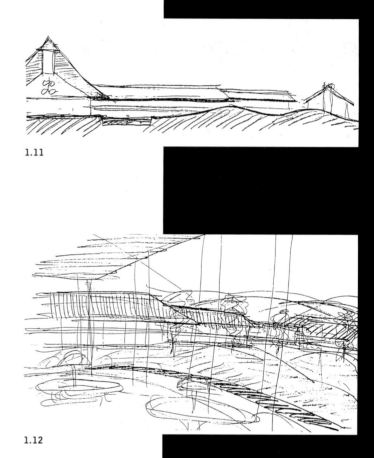

1.11

1.12

1.14

1.15 1st floor plan.
1.16 2nd floor plan.
1.17 Section of the
Community Hall.

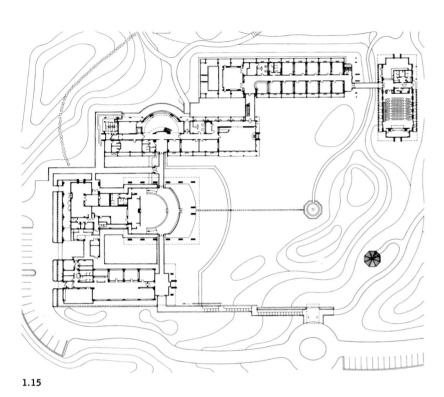

1.15

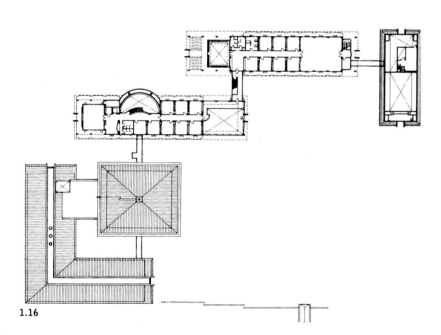

1.16

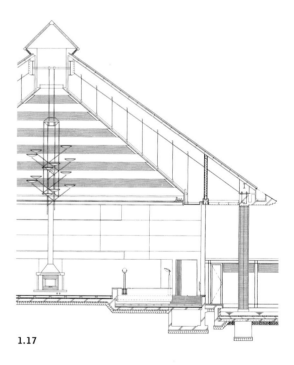

1.17

1.18 South elevation.
1.19 East elevation.
1.20 South–north section.

1.18

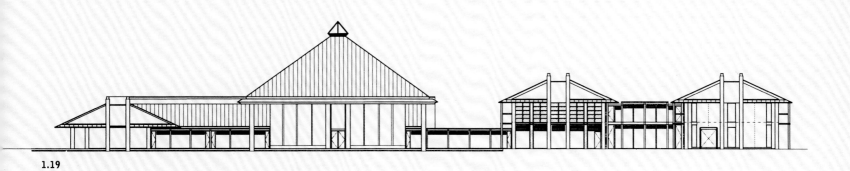

1.19

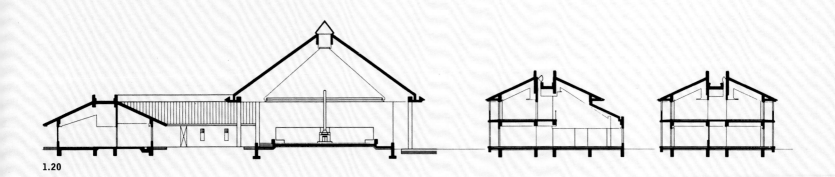

1.20

Kakegawa City Hall

Location:
Shizuoka Prefecture

Site area:
38,000 m²

Building area:
4,767 m²

Total floor area:
16,135 m²

Building purpose:
City hall

Number of floors:
+6, -1

Structure:
SRC, S

Completed:
1996

2.1 The city hall's atrium
showing the stepped levels and
public areas.

A City Hall in the Heartland

Kakegawa city is located in Shizuoka Prefecture—very close to the geographical heart of Japan. The old Tokaido highway that linked Kyoto with Edo (now Tokyo) conveyed many travellers of ancient times: among them itinerant engineers, journeymen architects, woodcarvers, and stone masons. (Almost half of the post towns depicted in the woodblock prints of *Fifty Three Stages of the Tokaido* by the artist Ando Hiroshige (1767–1858) are located in Shizuoka.)

The region enjoys a temperate climate and is the home of natural parks, fertile terraced plains and abundant lakes. Concealed by steep mountain ranges, streams surge from the ancient lava beds and the

waterways of the Oi and Tenryu rivers. The Prefecture is proud of its green tea production which provides Japan with over 46% of its tea crop. The resplendent emerald fields, fed by mineral-rich soils, add stunning definition to the slopes surrounding Kakegawa.

Civic unity and a new 'green' city hall are also a source of local pride. Despite its small town population, the city's residents have played a significant role in several major public initiatives. Funds mobilized by a citizen movement built the Shinkansen station to receive the bullet train from Tokyo, constructed the Tomei Expressway, and rehabilitated Kakegawa Castle. In all these enterprises the people of the city actively

participated in fund raising, planning, and project evaluation and design. This vital sense of community is embodied in the architecture of Kakegawa city hall.

The building is located approximately 2km west of the city centre, set into a hill close by the Tokaido Shinkansen train track. The natural elevation of the site suggested to the architects the creation of a park with the building as its centrepiece. In order to preserve the original topography, the setting was landscaped with islands of flowerbeds, and copses of dense trees clustered strategically to avoid creating a heat corridor around the perimeter. This arboreal barrier supports the innate cooling and ventilation functions of the building. As much as

possible, the cultivated surround reflects the natural flora of the locale, selected and planted appropriately to conserve indigenous animal habitats.

An Ecological Civic and Education Centre

Kakegawa city is one of the nation's leading municipalities in its promotion of lifelong learning. The city hall plays an important role in disseminating information on education programmes to the local community. The hall, which includes a designated educational area, creates a space that is 'open to the people, for use by the people'. It's a forum that allows visitors to encounter nature via the building's architecture while taking care of their civic business. Nikken Sekkei aimed

to create a civic centre that would dispense with any semblance of the traditional drab, forbidding government bureau. This structure would be aesthetically inviting with the layout allowing the citizen easy access to individual departments and public services. The project would promote and sustain local natural resources by successfully integrating state-of-the-art environmental technologies into the construction, and truly reflect the needs and concerns of both the municipal government and its citizenry.

The internal space of the city hall is dominated by an atrium that encompasses six floors. The extent mass of the atrium is enhanced dramatically by a series of stepped levels that comprise the public area of the

'Lifelong Education Terrace' and other facilities. On entering the building, the glass walls, combined with the atrium's height and the permeation of natural light, give the visitor a dramatic but inviting sense of volume. The learning terrace and the interior verandahs graduate the sun's entry to comfortable degrees. This is particularly evident when the day's luminance level is at its most intense. The airy, spacious atmosphere is further enhanced by a 360-degree view of the gardens and hills outside.

The layout and location of all the municipal departments can be seen and understood at a glance. The open-plan offices and reception desks for various public services are arranged along an 'engawa'

2.2 Site plan.
2.3 The approach to the main
entrance.
2.4 Aerial view with
surrounding topography and
the city hall set into the
hillside.
2.5 Close-up view of the
exterior.

2.3

2.4

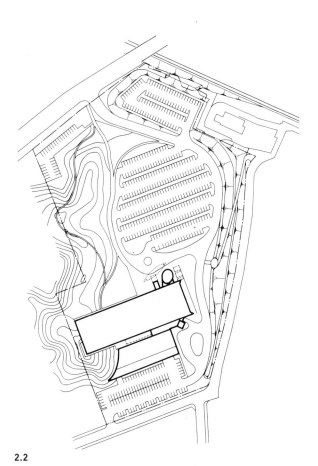

2.2

or verandah zone that encircles the entire atrium. This configuration facilitates communication among visitors and the staff.

Alleviation of Sunlight Loads

In most regions of Japan the sunlight from the west is the strongest and has the largest environmental load in most urban buildings. Countermeasures against this have always been a major challenge in building design. The plan for Kakegawa city hall was to locate the building on high ground west of the site, thus reducing the impact of solar glare. The height of the project was restricted to six floors that could be easily shaded by the western elevation. The building's form is a long east to west plane, minimizing the year-

round cooling load. Broad verandahs (engawas) diffuse the summer sun on the south façade and solar reflection from the roof is further decreased by the construction of a garden level atop a low-rise block.

The Engawa Corridor

A notable feature of the city hall's design is the use of the engawa (or verandah). In traditional Japanese architecture, this porch structure functioned as an open-air corridor that extended around a building to avoid placing inhabited rooms directly against exterior walls. It moderated the sun's glare, conveyed natural light and airflow to the interior, and acted as a buffer zone against severe weather conditions. The verandah

was also a social site for interchange among family members, and in receiving and entertaining guests. It extended the living space by allowing inhabitants an additional outside area to enjoy the garden while remaining sheltered. At Kakegawa city hall, the architects located the engawa inside the building, optimizing the floor area allocated to offices. They utilized the verandah's original attributes: social contact, natural air movement, moderated luminance and adaptable spaces to successfully integrate them into business sites.

Optimal Use of Sun, Rain and Natural Air Flow

The energy priorities of the project aim at significantly reducing electrical consumption

and the volume of mains water. Utilizing open-plan spaces and glass-clad walls allows an abundance of natural light to illuminate all areas of the city hall. In the verandah offices and the terrace levels of the atrium there is almost no need for artificial lighting during the building's normal opening hours.

In modern construction, it ought to be possible to cover all grey water needs with rainwater alone. Since Japan has always had an abundance of rain, this was a standard conservation factor of traditional buildings. (Shizuoka Prefecture has an average annual rainfall of 2360 mm.) At Kakegawa city hall, the rainwater is collected from the roof and used for toilet flushing, cooling tower replenishment, plant irrigation and other

applications. This method considerably reduces the volume of mains water used by the building.

Outside breezes are directed into the complex to an appropriate degree that maintains the indoor environment in the in-between seasons. Ventilation windows operated by remote control are located in the north and south faces of the atrium's peak.

The chimney effect generated by the height of the atrium draws in air via the ventilation windows of the first floor corridors, creating an airflow path through the extent of the office space. This air movement provides natural ventilation during the day, and cools the building at night. This active system achieves a substantial

reduction in the energy consumed for air conditioning.

The Functioning of a Green City Hall

The service zones of Kakegawa city hall are an open plan design. Nikken Sekkei thought this approach would create successful working systems with effective linkages between the different municipal departments. The plan also allows a flexible response to future structural changes. The deployment of offices is grouped according to function and each one clearly signposted. This enables members of the public to locate the service they're seeking easily.

In this area, the ordinary ceiling panel has been omitted to increase the height of the

2.6 Section detail.
2.7 Simulation of PPD.
2.8 The engawa corridor that
runs along the perimeter of
the city hall. This avoided
locating any inhabited rooms

directly against the exterior
walls. The concept is a pure
derivation from traditional
Japanese verandah design.
2.9 Service counter and office
area.

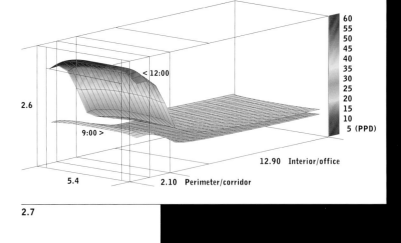

2.7

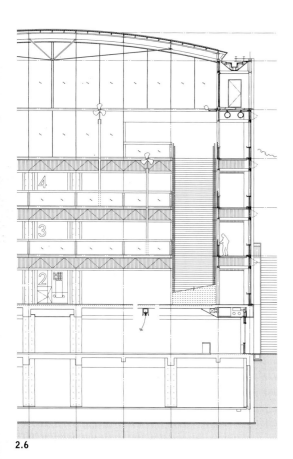

2.6

space. As there is no ceiling chamber,
the air conditioning ducts and light fixtures,
which are unified units, are fully exposed.
The floor is an OA floor, fully carpeted,
combining comfort with functionality.

The perimeter areas, which are
subject to exterior environmental loads, are
utilized for the verandah corridors, allowing
a stable environment in the inner work
zone. Air conditioning is divided between
equipment banks to process outside air
and apparatus above the ceiling of the
verandah corridors to handle interior thermal
loads. Ventilation-only air conditioning
between the heating and cooling seasons is
also possible.

Energy-saving Strategies in the Atrium

Artificial airflow in the atrium, which joins
the first four floors, combines ducted air
conditioning to the lower section and
the fifth-floor corridor, with a fan coil for
the Lifelong Education Terrace. When air
conditioning is used for cooling, it is
allocated to inhabited spaces only. Surplus
air from these areas passes through the
terrace, rising to the heat reservoir space at
the top of the atrium, where it is vented
from the building.

In the atrium corridors the hot air that
collects between the glass layers is allowed
to escape upwards through a slit. These
corridors do not require separate air conditioning equipment, except on the fifth floor.

When heat is required, the warm
air rises, leaving the terrace and other areas
prone to cold. This problem is alleviated
by the use of warm air recirculating ducts and
tall fans mounted on poles (an anti-frost
technology used on tea plantations), and also
for recirculation in reducing the vertical
temperature in the atrium to a few degrees.

During heat delivery, the excess air
from the working area is discharged from the
first floor, the reverse of the flow during
cooling. Local measures have been taken to
reduce cold draughts by the glazing of the
corridor. Baseboard heaters are installed
in the slit sections on the third floor and
underfloor heating is used on the first floor
and in the lobby. These energy-saving

2.8

2.9

solutions apply localized control within
a large area to achieve a successful balance
between comfort and economy.
(Architect: Shusaku Nanseki)

2.10 Schematic illustrating the distribution of natural light and airflow. Roof features include large mass area for rainwater collection storage tank and rooftop foliage to prevent reflective glare. The drawing also indicates parking, filter systems, sanitary facility, cooling tower, atrium, terrace and office area.
2.11 Airflow patterns drawing.
2.12 Detail of tall pole fans which are part of the ventilation system in the atrium. (Fans are the type used to aerate fields of the region's tea plantations.)
2.13 An experiment illustrating the variation in vertical temperature difference with the fan on and fan off.
2.14 View of levels 2,3 and 4 of the atrium.

2.12

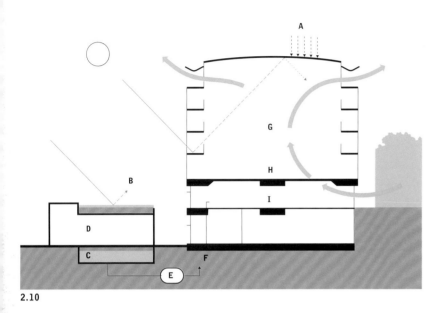

2.10

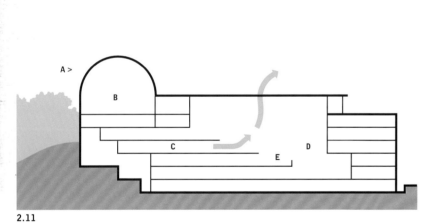

2.11

2.10
A Large roof for rain collection.
B Rooftop foliage to prevent reflected glare.
C Storage tank for rain water.
D Parking.
E Filter.
F Sanitary facility/cooling tower.
G Atrium.
H Terrace.
I Office area.

2.11
A Solar radiation from west.
B Assembly hall.
C Office area.
D Stepped atrium.
E Terrace.

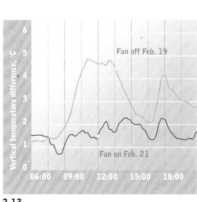

2.13

2.14

2.15 1st floor plan.
2.16 2nd floor plan.
2.17 6th floor plan.
2.18 Typical floor plan.

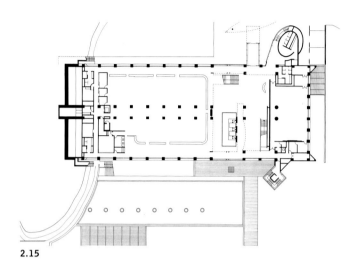

2.15

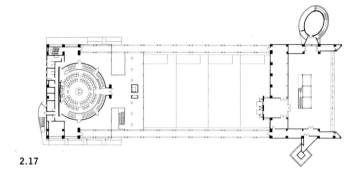

2.17

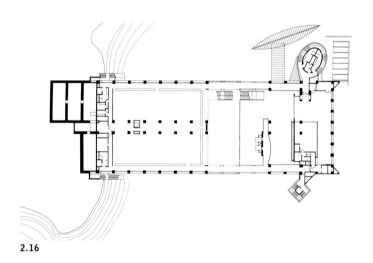

2.16

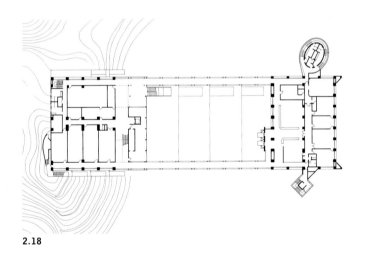

2.18

2.19 South–north section.
2.20 East–west section.
2.21 East elevation.
2.22 South elevation.
2.23 North elevation.

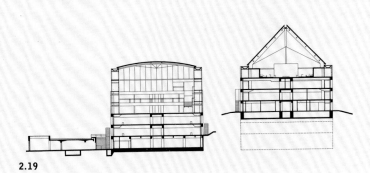

2.19

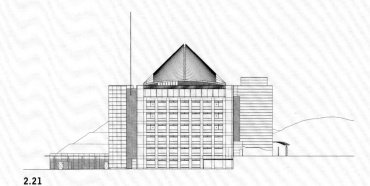

2.21

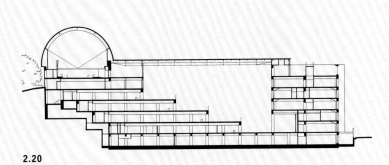

2.20

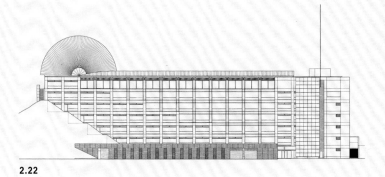

2.22

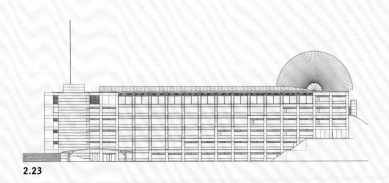

2.23

Izuna House

Location:
Nagano City

Site area:
3,597 m²

Building area:
608 m²

Total floor area:
990 m²

Building purpose:
Recreation facility

Number of floors:
+2, -1

Structure:
RC

Completed:
1991

3.1 View of the exterior
from the lounge with the
mobile wall partially raised.

Arcadia on the 'Roof of Japan'

Nagano Prefecture is situated at the centre of the island of Honshu, Japan's most populated landmass. The region possesses great natural beauty with a majestic alpine range formed by the Hida, Kiso and Akaishi Mountains. The calm grandeur of the Japanese Alps conceals many geological forces. Several of the snow-covered peaks are actually dormant or semi-active volcanoes that provide steam heat for volatile geysers and numerous hot spring spas (onsen) throughout the area. The region is also home to six national parks that offer year-round recreational activities. The 1998 Winter Olympics brought the Shinkansen (bullet train) to the area. The train and new super

highways have created closer ties with urban centres. Such access allows over 75,000 vacationers annually to escape the humidity of the cities for the Honshu Alps; to hike, climb and savour the healing mineral waters of the onsen.

North of the Prefecture's main city, also named Nagano, lies the southern highlands of Mt. Izuna, an area that could be called Japan's Arcadia. This idyllic setting of flowering meadows and lush forests of deciduous trees has an abundance of fishing ponds and deep sapphire-blue lakes fed by glacial waters from the Togakushi range. The highlands are also subject to severe weather conditions with snowfalls reaching from 60 cm to over 1 m.

Nikken Sekkei chose this pastoral location to build a mountain villa, whose architecture integrates and utilizes natural energy sources from the alpine environment. The complex functions as a rest and recreational facility that gives protection from the elements while incorporating nature both as an aesthetic and construction component. The two-storey structure, located at an altitude of 1100 m, is situated among gently undulating slopes that are restricted sites for vacation homes. Part of Chubu Mountains National Park, the highlands are a unique terrain with strong legal protections in place for indigenous plants and wildlife. Japan's building codes in national parks are equally strict with

regard to environmental standards, and
development is limited to specific zones.

A House to Catch the Wind
    In keeping with its mountain surroundings,
Izuna House was designed as an airy
sequence of open and closed spaces, a place
that would literally 'catch the wind'. The
project's energy mandate aimed at a
substantially reduced environmental impact,
restrained consumption of fossil fuels, and
minimal reliance on artificial cooling and
heating systems. Set deep in a thick stand
of trees, the composition of the facility
comprises a building for guest lodging and a
separate unit that houses a large kitchen
and other public quarters. These two areas
are connected by a common lounge that
has large mobile glass screens, which gives
the room spatial adaptability.
    Mountain topography influences
airflow in specific ways. Dense woodlands
around the Izuna site baffle the icy winds
from local glaciers. Similarly, the Izuna Villa
harnesses wind force from the highland
peaks via a series of architectural strategies
to cool dwelling spaces.
    Ancillary cooling is also supplied by
the forested perimeter. A tall corral of pines
rising above the roofline form a natural
enclosure, allowing shade and muted breezes
into the building. Multilevel pathways with a
7m difference at high and low points provide
a ventilation effect. Temperatures in these
'green' alleyways are further assisted by
plant transpiration.
    The lounge is a key component of
the building, an innovative feature elegant in
its simplicity and rewarding in its usage.
It's designed to function both as an interior
and exterior space. The single-storey room
is 10m by 8m in floor area and 6m in height.
On the north and south aspects there
are adjustable glass screens, 2m high by
8m wide that can be raised and lowered.
The screens, which form mobile walls, are
constructed of steel and glass on a grid
pattern. During warm summer days they're
raised to expose the room on both sides,
permitting cross ventilation from mountain
breezes. Unobstructed by walls, the visitor

3.2 Site plan.
3.3 Izuna House in winter.
3.4 Surrounding foliage helps
block direct sunlight.

3.5 A view from the garden
into the lounge. Mobile walls
on both the north and south
façades are partially raised to
allow cross ventilation.

3.3

3.4

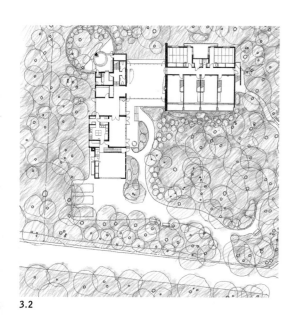

3.2

can experience the forest literally from their armchair. (Nature also brings in other 'guests'—woodland animals occasionally wander through the open lounge, attracted by the spatial access.)

In winter and at night when mountain temperatures plummet, the glass screens are lowered and the room becomes an interior again. This modulated space provides a sheltered platform permitting the dweller to experience nature in all its seasons.

Capturing natural breezes is also a feature of the guest quarters. The living facilities are located on three different levels, taking advantage of the site's sloping terrain. Bathrooms are situated on the lowest level, guestrooms on the second, while the upper

level is a recreational loft space. The upper and lower windows are 7m in height. The varying levels create a natural wind path, ventilating all the rooms without requiring conventional air conditioning. Even in the absence of winds, the cross ventilation is still effective owing to the different temperatures near the ceiling and the floor.

Nikken Sekkei examined the design for its viability and tested these effects using the latest Computer Fluid Dynamics technology. After the building was complete, actual measurements were taken to determine if efficient ventilation goals had been met. Air temperature and flow were monitored during summer nights in selected rooms with the windows left open.

Efficiency levels were compared to other rooms where the windows remained shut. The number of necessary ventilation times was determined at 4–6 times/h in terms of total room volume. The temperature difference between points near the windows on the uppermost levels and those on the lowest floor was 4–6 degrees centigrade. Wind measured outside on the balconies gave no evidence of impact. These values demonstrated that the temperature gradient ventilation using the distance between the highest and lowest windows realized the best efficiency.

In the daytime, a 10–20 times/h ventilation rate of total room volume was measured in rooms where the windows were

3.5

open. At the time of the actual assessment the wind speed on the balconies totalled 0.1–0.7 m/s. Thus, the wind power added a potency factor in the temperature gradient ventilation. The tests proved that in spaces where natural ventilation prevailed, even in summer, airflow was evenly distributed and room temperatures stayed cool, remaining below 26 degrees centigrade.

Channelling Heat from the Earth

Just as volcanic heat boils the fumaroles and hot springs of Mt. Chubu, Izuna House also successfully exploits geothermal energy via an 'earth' tunnel that's incorporated into the design. This heat and ventilation pathway uses outside air that's been slightly pre-cooled, channels it through a subterranean heat-storage unit and disperses the chilled flow into the living areas. (The geothermal tube also supplants the need to install a fossil fuel cooling method, which, at the Izuna villa, would only be required for a short time in the summer.) With solar glare much reduced by the broad eaves above the windows, and the room properly insulated from exterior heat, there is very little load on the innovative cooling system.

The 'earth' tunnel, a tube measuring 350 mm in diameter and 36 m in length, was buried 1.5 m beneath the garden. Using the earth's innate conductive properties, it cools the external air in summer and heats it in winter. The chilled air is pumped into the villa during the summer beneath the floors of the guestrooms. This method reduces the surface temperature of the floors to 22.5 degrees centigrade, giving the room a comfortable level of cooling. Results from performance measurements found that the temperature of the outside air was lowered from 28 degrees centigrade to 22 degrees centigrade, confirming that utilizing a local organic resource such as geothermal conduction was a more efficient clean energy alternative than fossil fuel.

Capturing the Wind and Sun
The Flexibility of an Airflow Roof

Solar heat is the main energy source for the villa and its use is expressed in the addition

3.6 Drawing illustrating the
path wind movement around
the house.

3.7 Lounge and view of the
exterior. The mobile walls
allow the space to be highly
adaptable to prevailing
climate conditions.

3.6

of a double-layered airflow roof whose
crests create a harmonious effect juxtaposed
against the triangular contours of
surrounding pines. The airflow roof has
dynamic insulating and conductive
properties. It was installed to collect solar
thermals via special glass panels for heating
water and inhabited spaces, and prevent
energy loading on the cooling system.

In the winter, fresh sun-warmed air
is captured by the southern eave and by the
air ducts in the 'earth' tunnel. It is then
supplied to various rooms.

During summer, air passes through
the two-layered roof and is carried away with
the exhaust air. This method maintains even
interior temperatures. The forces of land,
sun, mountain winds, sheltering forests
and heat from the earth's belly are built into
the very fabric of Izuna House. The villa
is a simple but sublime example of architects
thoroughly understanding the site of their
design, and how utilizing natural elements
can bring life to a building.
(Architect: Kazuya Ura)

3.8 Heat collection panel on the roof.
3.9 Solar shading in summer.
3.10 Solar radiation in winter.
3.11 Izuna's ventilation system in summer. Ventilation is provided by breezes cooled by shading foliage and outside air chilled in subterranean air ducts beneath the structure.
3.12 The ventilation system in winter. Outside air is warmed by heat collected from the roof and by the subterranean air ducts.
3.13 Section detail of heat collection panel.

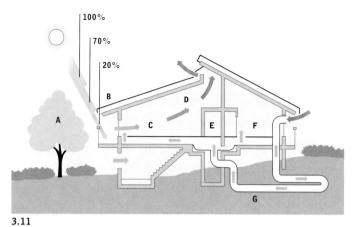

A Deciduous trees.
B Deep eaves.
C Bedrooms.
D Airflow path created.
E Corridor.
F Bedrooms.
G Cooling tube.

3.11

3.8

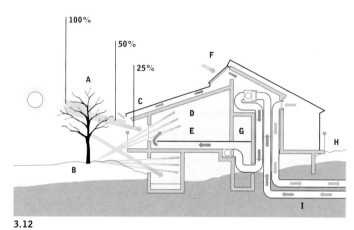

A Deciduous trees.
B Reflection from snow.
C Metal roof heat collector.
D Bedroom.
E Heated floor.
F Glass roof heat collector.
G Corridor.
H Snow acts as natural insulation.
I Heating tube.

3.12

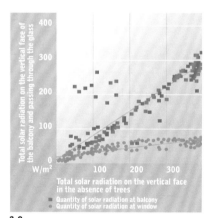

3.9

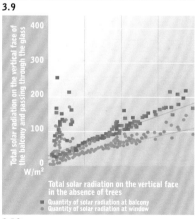

3.10

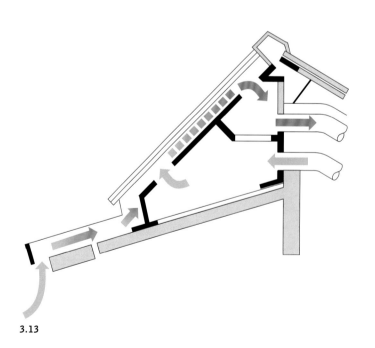

3.13

3.14 1st floor plan.
3.15 2nd floor plan.
3.16 1st basement floor.

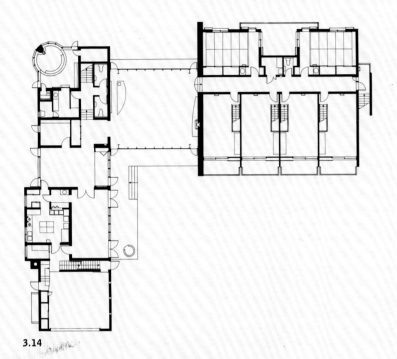

3.14

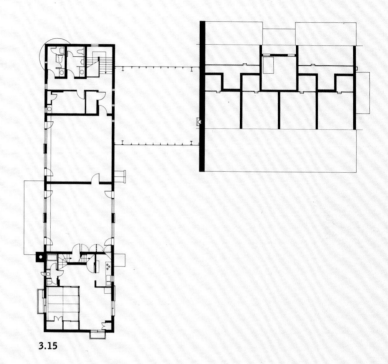

3.15

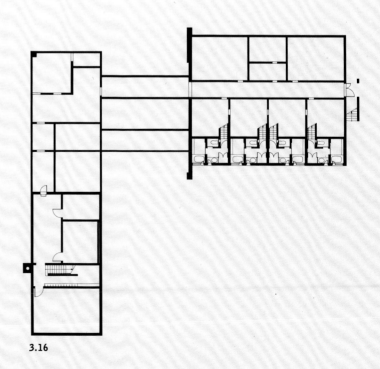

3.16

Konami Nasu Seminar House

Location:
Tochigi Prefecture

Site area:
5,977 m²

Building area:
977 m²

Total floor area:
2,415 m²

Building purpose:
Training facility

Number of floors:
+2, -1,

Structure:
RC

Completed:
1994

4.1 Night view. The entrance
to Konami/Nasu Seminar
House located on the top floor.

Building in the Ring of Fire

Sprung from the molten fires of composite volcanoes, the Nasu Highlands of north-eastern Honshu present a rugged and imposing wilderness. Calm enough at present to allow thick groves of cedars to flourish on their slopes, the range is part of the Nikko-Nasu National Park. The region encompasses 3200 square kilometres of cambered mountains and forested plateaux. Its close proximity to Tokyo makes it a major year-round resort area of Tochigi Prefecture.

A House Embedded in a Hill

The Konami Company was first established as an amusement machine manufacturer in Osaka in 1965. Today, it has successfully evolved into a total computer entertainment enterprise with a wide range of computer and video game products. In 1998, it became a publicly traded company in Tokyo with 2000 employees worldwide. The Konami Seminar House was built to provide a pleasant venue where the staff could come for training courses and bring their families.

The Seminar House, located halfway up the Nasu range, was designed in accord with the natural forms of the surrounding topography. The site parallels a main highway, measuring 45m from north to south and approximately 135m from east to west. A wide border of trees and plants protects the building's frontage from the road and the noisy intrusion of traffic. A further barrier is created by a central parking lot encircled by the drive leading to the main entrance.

The House form, with its magnificent views, is truly a child of the hill in which it lies anchored. The site declines steeply to the south, its undulations continuing on to the Kanto plain. To reduce the surface profile and overall bulk, the architects of Nikken Sekkei chose to follow the angle of the slope by embedding half of the building's volume into the earth. The remaining extrusion faces south before a descending lawn leading to dense woodlands.

The roof rises above the entrance and a unique series of glass baffles form a transparent corridor. Projecting from one

side of this configuration is a cantilevered steel canopy, designed from a wind motif, whose sharp profile is visible from the surrounding valley. The eastern roof space supports a green surface planted with trees and flowers matching the height of the adjacent tree line.

The lounge, restaurant and other public spaces are located on the second floor of the west façade. Glass walls in these areas look out onto impressive views of the Nasu peaks. The training department and playrooms are located on the floor below. Guestrooms, bath and toilet facilities and other private areas are housed in the east wing, on the first and second floors. The guest quarters are deliberately positioned at

ground level along the south wall to provide an expansive view of the foothills of the Nasu highlands. The water supply for bathrooms in the residential wing is heated by solar power using vacuum tube-type heat collectors. The sun also provides heat for other grey water uses. Solar power reduces the facility's energy consumption by 46%.

An access corridor extending along the north aspect of the building links all the rooms. Imaginative use of concrete and glass gives this multilevel avenue subtle shifts of sunlight and shadow. Skilfully combining building materials also allows it to function as a conduit of heat and ventilation. The walls are made of thick concrete, creating a Trombe's wall, while the roof has a canopy of

highly insulating Low-ε glass. Part of the corridor lies below the surface level and light is delivered through the overhead cladding and a series of tall slit windows that encompass two floors. This configuration allows the walkway and staircases to be naturally illuminated for most of the day. The windows in the corridors open outward for ventilation and seating islands are arranged at strategically sunny spots in the lounge space where residents can meet and relax with each other.

The height of the corridor produces a gravity ventilation effect and its design was determined through the use of simulations. In summer, the concrete effacement absorbs the sun's heat, increasing air temperatures

4.2 Site plan.
4.3 The entrance canopy designed as a wind motif.
4.4 Aerial view of the Seminar House and the surrounding landscape.
4.5 Glass wind baffles.

4.3

4.4

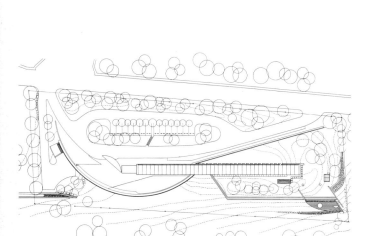

4.2

under the roof's canopy. This hot air is allowed to escape through vents to be replaced by cooler air drawn in from outside. During winter the concrete insulation accumulates and retains heat, keeping the corridor warm without resorting to the use of fossil fuels.

The Earth as an Insulator

The concept of sinking part of the building's mass into the hill utilizes the innate cooling and warming properties of the earth. Just as in a cave, earthen temperatures vary little throughout the year. Nikken Sekkei further exploited the natural attributes of the site by creating a system whereby air could exchange heat with the soil. This conversion was achieved through geo-engineering a complex of heating and cooling tubes buried beneath the House. As a result, fresh air entering the building is warmed by the soil in winter and cooled by it in summer. This leads to a substantial saving in fossil energy consumed by the building. When the plan's engineers ran energy assessments, the past performance tests showed that the successful combination of natural and mechanical ventilation provided the guest rooms on the first floor with a comfortable temperature range of 22 to 26 degrees centigrade.

(Architect: Kiyoshi Sakurai)

4.6 Thermal environment
simulation of the guest room
corridors in winter.
4.7 Air temperature
distribution in the corridor
during a sunny day in winter.

4.8 Walls constructed from
coloured concrete.
4.9 A view of the corridor
from the baffle windows.

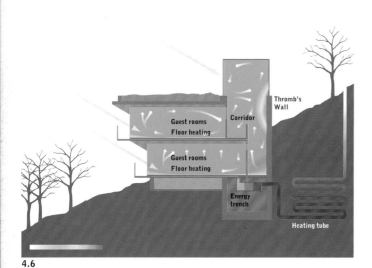

4.6

4.8

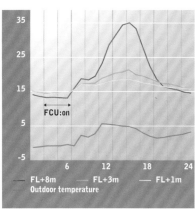

4.7

4.9

4.10 Thermal environment
simulation in summer.
4.11 Air temperature of the
corridor and guest rooms on a
summer day with the windows
closed.
4.12 Air temperature of the
corridor and guest rooms on a
summer day with the windows
open.

4.13 A long view of the
corridor.
4.14 The second floor dining
room.
4.15 Ventilation windows
along the roof of the corridor.

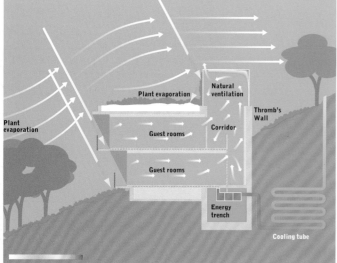

4.10

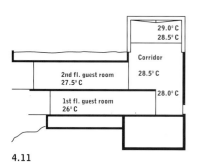

4.11

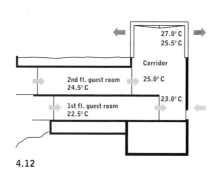

4.12

4.13

4.14

4.15

4.16 Sectional sketch.
4.17 Site plan sketch.
4.18 Taking natural energy
to the building.

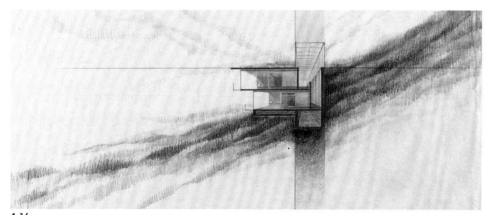

4.16

4.17

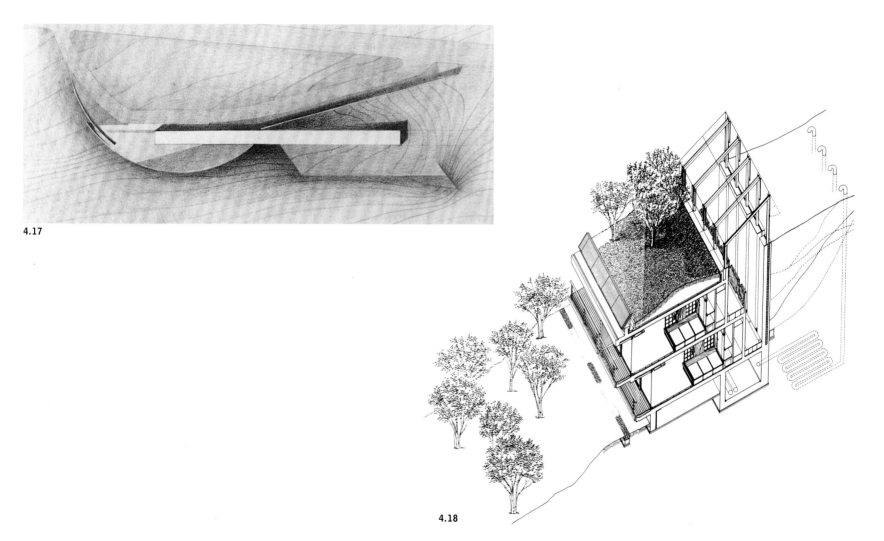

4.18

4.19 1st floor plan.
4.20 2nd floor plan.
4.21 Axonometric drawing.

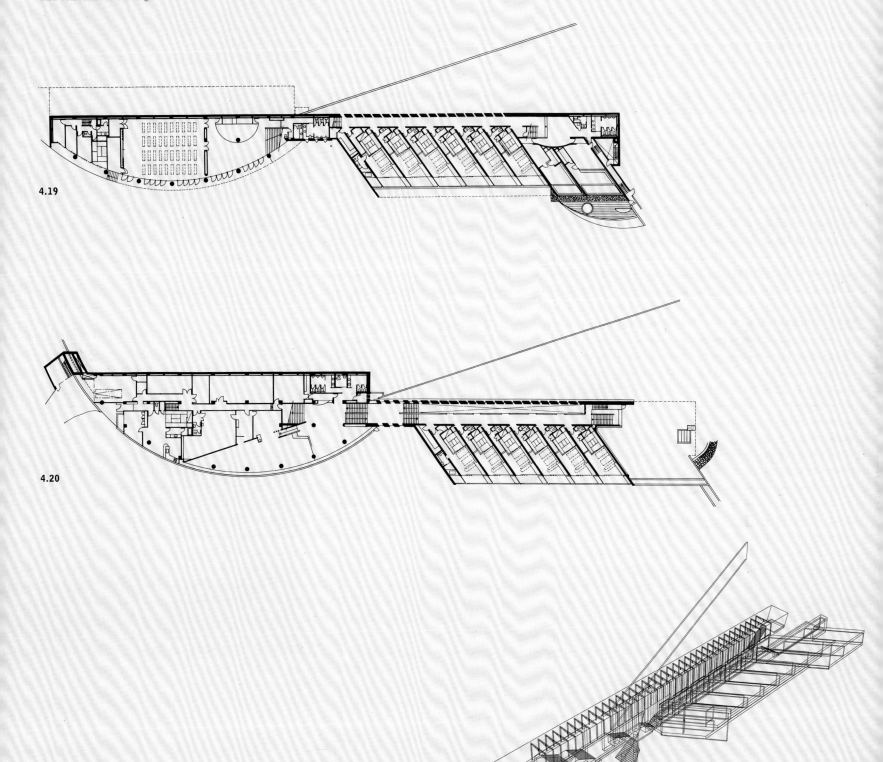

4.19

4.20

4.21

JICA Hokkaido International Centre Obihiro

Location:
Obihiro City, Hokkaido

Site area:
4,391 m²

Building area:
2,132 m²

Total floor area:
4,400 m²

Building purpose:
Training facility

Number of floors:
+3, -1

Structure:
RC

Completed:
1996

5.1 Residence wing and
balconies viewed from the
courtyard.

Building a Centre for International Understanding

Hokkaido is the second largest and most northern of the four main islands of Japan. Local weather patterns are influenced by the marine triangle of the Seas of Okhotsk, Japan and the Pacific, creating many months of harsh winter offset by cool, comfortable summers. The region is home to several rare bio-environments and unique wilderness sites, from the Jozankei Gorge to the Kushiro Swamps. Daisetsu National Park and its mountains comprise the backbone of the island. It is a prominent dairy and crop-farming centre, with farms run on an extensive scale.

Located at a latitude of 43 degrees north, the city of Obihiro is renowned for the beauty of its scenery. During winter, cold air masses move down from Siberia and the temperatures drop to –20 degrees centigrade while summer temperatures can reach over 30 degrees centigrade.

Obihiro is one of the homes of the Japan International Cooperation Agency (JICA) which implements the programmes of the Official Development Assistance (ODA). JICA/Hokkaido International Centre Obihiro is the 11th such training centre and is founded on 'human development, national development and unity among people'. The Centre's major focus is 'technology and knowledge transfer', its programmes provide technical training, research, and disaster relief to needy communities worldwide.

As its first principle, the ODA Charter of 1992 cites that environmental conservation and social–economic development should be practised in partnerships among member nations across the globe. With this in mind, Nikken Sekkei designed the JICA building to exist in complete reciprocity and harmony with its natural surroundings and to function as a housing facility for trainees from developing countries worldwide. The Centre is on a forested hill site above Obihiro, in a city park area covering 405 hectares.

Between Earth and Sky

The immediate landscape is a dramatic vista of dark green forests and broad plains reaching to distant mountains beneath a vast

expansive sky. Given this backdrop, the architects avoided a structure that would impose. Rather, they conceived the building as a discreet architectural form that leaves the intrinsic features of the site unchanged. The design is an elegant, low-lying building plan with clean, simple lines, positioned in an arbour of Japanese northern pines. Part of the exterior pays tribute to the abundant variety of native trees by using timbers from a local fir species called todo-matsu.

The facility receives a large number of trainees from partner nations every year. Many of these guests are absent from their home countries for the first time. It was important to create a space that would be inviting and peaceful, where the residents could return from a day's training on the outside to a supportive and serene atmosphere.

The Centre is comprised of a three-storey main building with an adjacent single level unit parallel to it. Between the buildings is a sunny courtyard that has paved areas shaded by birch trees. The primary structure is organized as two long wings that function as the residential space, with bedrooms on the second and third floors, each with a private balcony. Two glass stairwells provide a major light source from the east to the west boundary of the facility. The roof rises to a peak above the residence and contains solar collecting panels. An entrance lobby connects the main area with the lower building that accommodates the lounge and the dining room. This section has a colonnaded verandah (gangi) on the west façade while its northern aspect faces the inner courtyard. Clean energy sources from solar power; wind airflow and geothermal heat sustain the Centre's physical plant.

Utilizing the Heat of the Earth

Local weather extremes posed an initial problem of heating and cooling the buildings, in terms of both cost and environmental concerns. The main facility, because of heavy human traffic, requires ample ventilation. The solution was to make effective use of Obihiro's climate by taking advantage of geothermal energy beneath the site.

5.2 Site plan.
5.3 JICA – external view.
5.4 West façade – the
'engawa' balcony in the dining
and lounge area. Solar
collectors are visible on the
roof.

5.5 The second floor balcony.
5.6 The courtyard.
5.7 Stair towers span three
floors and function as both
airflow and light conduits.

5.3

5.4

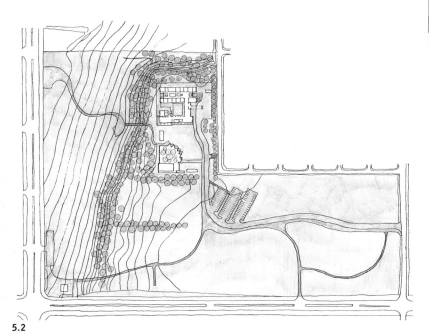

5.2

5.5

Nikken Sekkei, expanding on their earlier success with geothermal technology, constructed a huge subterranean energy-gathering system that is one of the largest of its type in Japan. A heat-collecting tube 60 cm in diameter and 230 m in total length was sunk into earth under the foundation. Via this method, fresh air could be pre-warmed or pre-cooled and delivered through the air conditioning unit to ventilate all parts of the Centre. Since geothermal heat varies only slightly throughout the year, the system operates without being affected by the weather and diverse surface temperatures.

Post-construction analysis demonstrated that, by using this energy system, summer temperatures of 34 degrees centigrade were cooled to 22 degrees, and winter temperatures of –10 degrees centigrade were raised to –3 degrees . This greatly reduced the need for reliance on fossil fuels. According to measurements recorded at the site in 1996, the lowest temperature occurred in February, –19 degrees centigrade, while the highest outside temperature in May and July was 34 degrees centigrade. In contrast, at the depth at which the tube was buried, the variation was only 9–19 degrees centigrade. This differential is used to preheat the outside air in winter and cool it in the summer.

Using Solar Energy at JICA

The metal roof of the main building is two-layered with special insets on its western slope for solar panels. Sunlight is concentrated through the glass cells at points where the rays are at their most intense. This pre-warms the outside air for the heating ducts. The hot air is then delivered into the ventilation system from one end of the roof crest. This allows it to pre-heat –10 degrees centigrade air to 5 degrees.

Based on analyses and tests, Nikken Sekkei was able to make fairly accurate estimates on the costs savings in energy consumption by using geothermal and solar power. Consumption was only 38 % compared to what the usage levels would be if fossil fuels were used. Tapping into natural energy sources also lowered the petroleum fuel

5.6

5.7

consumption in the summer by 29%. These results show that pre-processing of outside air before bringing it into the ventilation/air conditioning system is an extremely valuable strategy, with benefits both for the Centre's budget and its immediate environment.

Towers of Wind, Eaves of Glass and the Return of the Gangi

Glass is utilized throughout the building for both energy delivery and aesthetic purposes. Glass eaves cover the balconies of the dormitory rooms. As well as cutting off the sun's rays to some extent, they reflect light into the rooms, give protection against the rain and sleet, and prevent snow from building up on the balconies.

Both the north and south ends of the dormitory facility are entry/exit areas flanked by two stairwells on either side. The stair 'towers' are capped with glass and have windows that span three floors. The Centre's residents and staff consider them to be 'towers of light' because they allow the sun to penetrate deep into the interior of the building. Apart from providing bright and open staircases, the towers also function as conduits of airflow. In summer, and in the changing periods of each season, the windows on the tower caps and on the first floor are opened. This creates natural vertical ventilation and helps to keep the public spaces cool. In addition, during the winter, the concrete walls of the stairwells store heat

from the sun and raise the efficiency of the heating system. The concrete walls of the stairwells function as Thromb's walls.

In the first-floor lounge and dining room on the west side of the building, a belt of under-roof deck space about 1.8m wide separates the windows from direct exposure to the elements. This feature, called gangi, is borrowed from traditional designs used in areas such as Niigata that are prone to heavy blizzards.
(Architect: Ataru Tsuchiya)

5.8 Glass stair tower permits entry of abundant light and creates natural ventilation when the vents in the apex of the tower and on the first floor are open.

5.9 Air vents situated at floor level.
5.10 Air vents on the first floor.
5.11 The dining room.
5.12 The 'engawa' space on the first floor.

5.9

5.10

5.8

5.11

5.12

5.13 Effects of the cooling
and heating tube in winter.
5.14 Effects of the solar
collectors in winter.

5.15 Schematic of the
building showing function and
allocation of the cooling and
heating tube and the solar
collectors.

A Solar heat and air heat
collector (2 outside air
conditioners).
Glass-covered section: 135 m²
4,700 to 12,250 m³/h [0.03
to 0.01 m (m³/h)].
B Tower for wind and light.
C Guest rooms, seminar
rooms, offices, etc.
D Entrance hall.
E Wooden brick footway.
F Interlocking blocks
driveway.
G Duct pit ventilation using
surplus vented air.
H Storm water receiver for
water closet: 110 m³
Roof area: 2,100 m²
(0.05 m³/m²).
I Subterranean
cooling/heating tubes
(1 outside air conditioners).
Circuit through guest rooms.
Polyvinyl chloride pipes 0.6 m
ø x 41 m (77 m²).
J Outside air volume control.
3,700 m³/h [0.02 m² (m³/h)].
K Subterranean
cooling/heating tubes
(2 outside air conditioners).
Office and seminar room
circuit.
Polyvinyl chloride pipes 0.6 m
ø x 131 m (247 m²).
L Outside air volume control
1,000 to 8,550 m³/h [0.25 to
0.03 m² (m³/h)].
M Subterranean
cooling/heating tubes
(3 outside air conditioners).
Lounge and dining room
circuit.
Polyvinyl chloride pipes 0.6 m
ø x 51 m (96m²).
N Outside air volume control
1,680 to 3,500 m³/h
[0.04 to 0.03 m² (m³/h)].
O The subterranean
cooling/heating tubes are
buried along the foundation.
P Wooden deck.
Q Lounge and dining room.
Warm air floor heating.
Double layered wooden floor.
Non-CFC foamed insulating
material.
R Wooden sash windows,
double glazed, insulative and
airtight.
S Wooden balcony.
T Solar heat and air heat
collector (3 outside air
conditioners).
Metal roof section 402 m²+.
Glass-covered roof 58 m² =
460 m²
1,680 to 3,500 m³/h [0.27 to
0.13 m² (m³/h)].
U Light and wind tower.
Northern staircase with high
sidelights on the southwest
side.

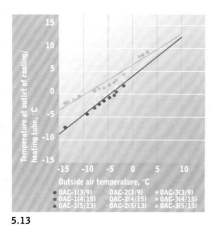

5.13

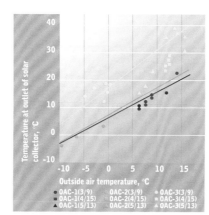

5.14

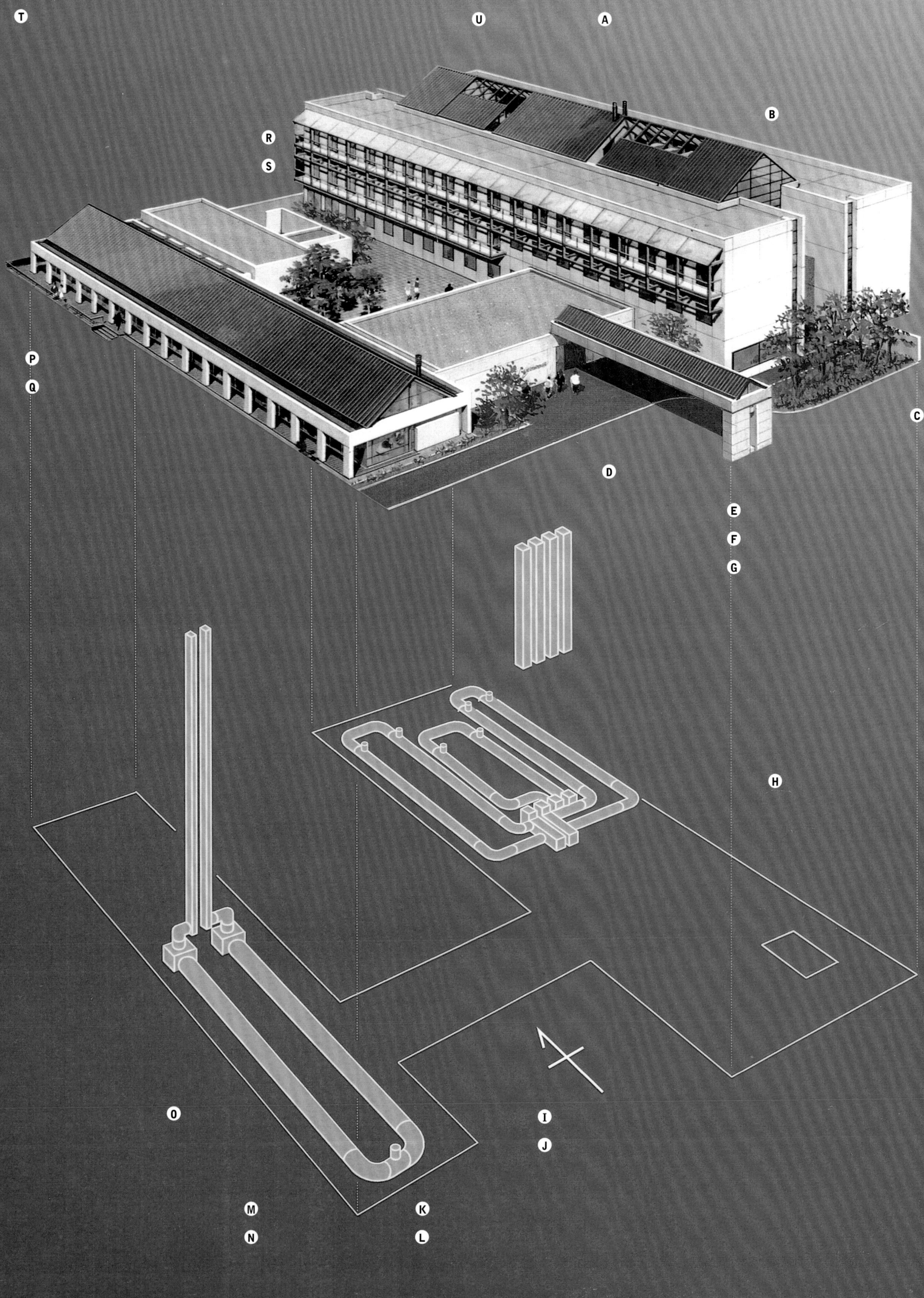
T
U
A
B
R
S
P
Q
C
D
E
F
G
H
O
I
J
M
K
N
L

5.16 The building's oil consumption rates proving a 38% reduction rate in winter and a 29% reduction in summer.

5.17 The air ventilation system in the stair towers.
5.18 The roof's heat collecting system.

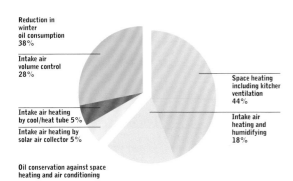

Reduction in winter oil consumption 38%

Intake air volume control 28%

Intake air heating by cool/heat tube 5%

Intake air heating by solar air collector 5%

Space heating including kitcher ventilation 44%

Intake air heating and humidifying 18%

Oil conservation against space heating and air conditioning

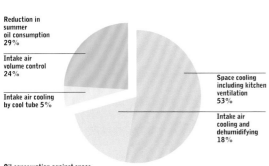

Reduction in summer oil consumption 29%

Intake air volume control 24%

Intake air cooling by cool tube 5%

Space cooling including kitchen ventilation 53%

Intake air cooling and dehumidifying 18%

Oil conservation against space cooling and air conditioning

5.16

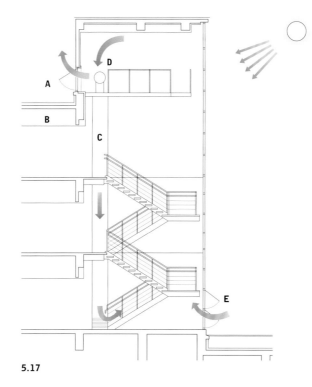

A Ventilation opening.
B Direct gain.
C Duct.
D A fan sends warmed air to the first floor.
E Ventilation opening.

5.17

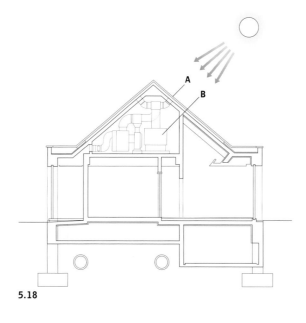

A Heat-collecting roof.
B Air conditioner.

5.18

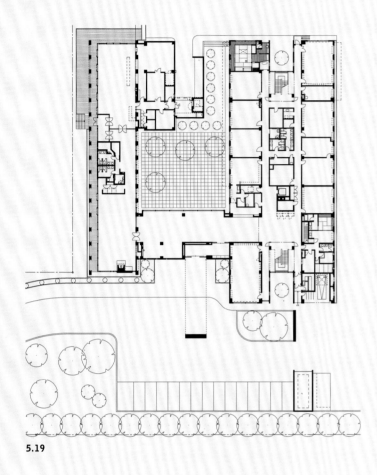

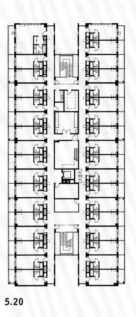

5.20

5.19

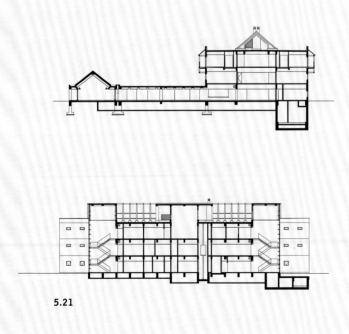

5.21

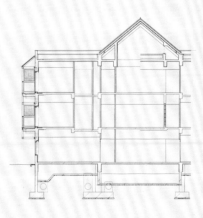

5.22

Lake Biwa Museum and UNEP International Environmental Technology Centre

Lake Biwa Museum

Location:
Shiga Prefecture

Site area:
42,433 m²

Building area:
13,208 m²

Total floor area:
25,239 m²

Use of the building:
Museum

Number of floors:
+2, −1

Structure:
SRC, RC, S

Completed:
1996

UNEP International
Environmental Technology
Centre

Site area:
12,718 m²

Building area:
2,610 m²

Total floor area:
3,017 m²

Use of the building:
Office, lodgings

Number of floors:
+2, −1

Structure:
RC, S

Completed:
1995

Co-architect (both projects):
Shiga Prefectural Government

6.1 The crescent-shaped roof of the museum is inspired by the design of 'maruko' boats, formerly the most common vessel to sail on Lake Biwa.

Partnered in Nature

The Karasuma Peninsula in Shiga Prefecture is a spine of rock and silt stretching out across the vast expanse of Lake Biwa. Two major ecological institutions stand together on the broad span as part of a comprehensive building plan: the Lake Biwa Museum and the UNEP International Environmental Technology Centre Shiga. Situated on a 'super-block' 54,000 square metres in size, the buildings are designed to be recumbent on the site and blend into the backdrop of the lake.

Lake Biwa is Japan's largest freshwater lake and one of the world's most prehistoric bodies of water. As an architectural site, this immense waterway captures on its mirrored surface the roofline of long-settled communities bordered by the shoulders of distant mountains. Its fertile banks allowed the architects to include a cultivated 'Water and Greenery' promenade which runs along the edge of the Museum and the UNEP Centre forming a common garden area, connecting the boat landing with a water plant park.

The total volume of the buildings' height was kept as low as possible to impart a sense of order and give emphasis to the horizon by clustering them into a harmonious group. To reaffirm their scale and unity, a free-standing wall of stoneware tile was built along the promenade, bearing a design unifying water, rock and earth. The entrance to each building is accessed via the gardens, a pleasant traverse that, at each complex, envelops the visitor immediately in a close panoramic view of the lake.

In Praise of Water – Lake Biwa and the Museum Complex

Encompassing 679 square kilometres with a water load of over 27.5 billion gallons, Lake Biwa is the premier watershed for the nearby communities of Kusatsu City. Witness to 4 million years of evolution, this ancient reservoir and its shores are rich in natural vegetation and wildlife. Many organisms that survive here exist nowhere else in the world. During the Edo period, Lake Biwa was an important transportation artery between the cities of Kyoto and Osaka. Such an

accessible trade and information route allowed for the growth of a rich waterside culture and many diverse human settlements have left their history on its banks. Their descendants still farm and fish the area. Despite encroaching ecological conflicts, Lake Biwa sustains the entire Yodogawa river network along with the 14 million residents of the Kansai region.

Complex in its hydrodynamics and multifaceted in its capacities, the lake is home to unique and rare bio-strata, from the minute rock snail and tiny marsh violet to five-foot long catfish and lotus flowers the size of dinner plates. The Lake Biwa Museum, opened in 1996, is located on the eastern shore. Its major purpose is to preserve and

research the relationship between the community, the shore environment and this vast body of fresh water. Exhibits here incorporate Biwa's many roles as the great Aqua Mater. However, the Museum's scope is not limited to local concerns. Its scientific study programmes also include lakes and marshes in the rest of Asia and around the globe. By conducting research of international significance at Lake Biwa, the Museum aims to contribute to the growing body of knowledge concerning biological diversity, indigenous waterside cultures, and the urgent need to preserve fresh water resources world-wide.

Given the scope of the site, the first instinct of the architects was to keep the

buildings aligned with the local topography and reduce any disturbance of the site's natural beauty. The museum has two storeys above ground and one floor underground, with a total floor space covering approximately 25,000 square metres. A sweeping, crescent-shaped roof resembling a ship's hull affords the museum deep eaves as a shield against summer heat. The roof's design is derived from the 'maruko' boat, once the most common sailing vessel on Lake Biwa.

Anchored to the roof are 9–12m high massive glass windows secured by stainless steel fittings based on a tension mullion structure. These glass walls enclose a permanent display area, a plan display room,

6.2 Site plan of the Lake Biwa Museum and the UNEP complex.
6.3 View of the Museum and UNEP complex from across Lake Biwa.
6.4 Aerial view of the buildings.

6.5 Distant view showing the site's location on the lake's banks.
6.6 The circular exhibition hall (the aquarium building) with the reflecting pond fed by Lake Biwa.

6.3

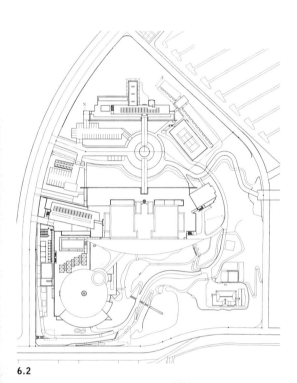

6.2

6.4

restaurant, museum shop, library and the experiential learning room. The museum's atrium lobby extends deeply into the building, allowing indirect, soft natural light to enter at many points. The vaulted roof has a layer of glass beneath which lies a series of artificial lights with louvres that are activated at night to provide luminance.

Corridors from the atrium connect the lakeside of the building where there is a round, two-level hall that hosts many exhibitions on the lifecycles of Biwa's environment. This exhibition hall has a dome-shaped ceiling with natural light brought from side lights and top lights. When the sidelights are slid open, natural ventilation becomes possible.

Building with Water

Nikken Sekkei's design honours Lake Biwa in all its aspects by literally integrating it into the museum. Lake water is a key component in the architectural scheme and is utilized everywhere. It plays in landscaped rivulets around the entrance gardens, collects in exhibition ponds and runs musically beneath archways. It rests in shining pools to reflect the expanse of glass walls and streams alongside connecting walkways and jetties. A dynamic rendering of lake life exists where it flows into an underground freshwater aquarium on the first floor. The aquarium holds 950 tonnes of water and 180 different kinds of fish, making it one of the largest freshwater piscine exhibits in Japan. The

huge tank is designed as a facsimile of Biwa's natural submerged terrain and water for the aquatic animals is pumped into the artificial habitat from 300m out in the lake. Illumination inside the aquarium accurately simulates the sun-filtered green glow of the lake's depths. This is achieved through a special lighting system and a sunlight tracking device that not only helps the aquatic plants to grow, but also provides the fish with an artificial 'day'. Visitors experience the dramatic effect of being enveloped by this watery kingdom as they view the fish from inside a glass tunnel that penetrates the aquarium's core.

To the delight of children, a 'Touching Pool' was added where they can view and gently handle species of fish that dwell in the

6.5

6.6

shallows. More life beneath Biwa's waves can be found at the outdoor exhibition space which includes a biotope pond. This live exhibit area highlights the flora and fauna that exist on the surrounding shores. The pond, constructed with varying levels of sunken terraces, displays the rich plant and animal life that flourish within the lake.

Curating a Finite Resource

Naturally, the museum is a prime model in water recycling and conservation. The water system, for both domestic and exhibition use, has many safeguards in place to avert invasive contaminants. The gallons drawn into the aquarium are used as lab samples and are tested daily for pollutants.

To prevent wastewater from the facilities polluting the lake was a major consideration. It was decided to pave as little of the complex as possible. Much of the ground surface was planted with shallow root plants or grassed walkways to create maximum rainwater absorption. After being treated by being percolated through a pebble bed, the water is returned to the lake. The remaining run-off, both from the museum and the adjacent UNEP International Environmental Technology Centre building, is collected, filtered and recycled for multiple purposes; replenishing garden ponds and water exhibits, spraying the grounds and rooftops for cooling purposes, and for the toilet facilities.

The UNEP Building Complex

An appropriate companion building to the Lake Biwa Museum, the United Nations' Environmental Programme Centre works to encourage national and global partnerships in sustaining the environments of cities and suburbs in relation to freshwater lakes and water resources. Its programmes inform and educate communities on how to improve the quality of their urban and natural habitats without imposing environmental and water deficits on future generations.

The library of the UNEP International Environmental Technology Centre has a two-level light well. Wooden eaves 2m deep positioned at 2.3m from the floor effectively block out the sun. Double-glazed glass,

6.7 Solar collectors and the
sun-tracking mechanism on
the Museum's roof.
6.8 The pedestrian viewing
tunnel running beneath the
aquarium.

6.7

90 cm by 90 cm thick, in composite layers of
hollow, white polycarbonate lattice was
installed in the upper portion of the eaves.
This approach provides excellent insulation
and produces a soft lighting effect similar
to that of traditional Japanese shoji screens
(sliding paper-lattice doors). The middle
of the light well houses a top light that can be
opened to release warm air produced by
natural ventilation.

Natural Technologies and the Interior Climate
At the UNEP lodging facility, the design
incorporated a number of sustainable
technologies in order to maintain an optimum
interior climate. They included a strategically
distributed natural ventilation network, solar

heat and solar-powered air conditioning,
large and small scale entry points for natural
light, geothermal energy for both heat and
ventilation, and an exterior sprinkler system
that uses collected rainwater to spray the
roofs in hot weather.

The architectural mandate was to use
natural energy as much as possible. In the
case of the residential units, this required
reconsidering the temperature ranges as cool
vs. warm instead of hot vs. cold. For example,
in the summer, instead of setting the upper
temperature limit at 26 degrees centigrade,
it's kept at 28 degrees, based on the idea
that any temperature even slightly below this
will feel 'cool' by comparison. These basic
principles have a long tradition in Japan as

organic methods to balance room
temperatures. Revisited and utilized here in
the UNEP complex, they provide very
comfortable warmth and cooling levels for
everyday living.

Eaves, Trees, Solar Heat and Rainwater
Effective use of natural resources requires
minimizing the load on the building's
energy core. At the UNEP facilities, wall
insulation and double-glazing were used to
maximize weatherproofing. Wood fibre
cement plates for both the wall mouldings
and frame were constructed with timber from
thinned-out forests. The balconies were
designed with deep eaves positioned at the
highest level of the surrounding deciduous

6.8

trees. These two elements combine to keep out intense sunlight. During winter, when the trees shed their leaves, the sun's low position on the horizon allows light to penetrate the building through the branches and under the eaves.

A key problem in preventing the sun from heating up the roof and penetrating the building was solved by use of an airflow surface. This method attracts hot air, channelling it from one side of the roof, extracting the heat and then expelling it from the other side. The temperature of this air layer is detected by a sensing mechanism that triggers, as necessary, automatic sprays of accumulated rainwater all over the roof's surface to bring down the temperature.

Energy from the Sun and the Earth

The floor design throughout the facility was aimed at heightening the radiation effect. A floor heating system that utilizes air warmed by solar power was installed beneath a raised floor. The air supplied to each room is transported beneath the extent of the floor's surface. This has the effect of cooling the floor in summer and heating it in winter months, thus maintaining an appropriate temperature level through all the rooms year round. During particularly severe weather the radiation effect from the floor can be elevated to maintain all spaces at a comfortable and liveable temperature. Another strategy used in lowering the heat load and cooling the facility, without resorting to refrigeration,

involved the construction of a subterranean wind tube buried beneath the complex. This works by using underground water to cool the outside air before supplying it to the rooms. Ground water is pumped up into a cooling coil which extracts the heat from the air. Thereafter, the water, which is drawn from a well fed by Lake Biwa and sunk almost 90 m underground, is recycled and returned to the aquifer.

(Architect: Katsuya Kawashima)

6.9 Schematic of how water
from Lake Biwa enters the
building and is dispersed
throughout the Museum.
6.10 View of the Museum's
west façade.

6.11 The Museum's northern
façade. Earth coloured tiles
are used to harmonize the
building's surroundings.

6.10

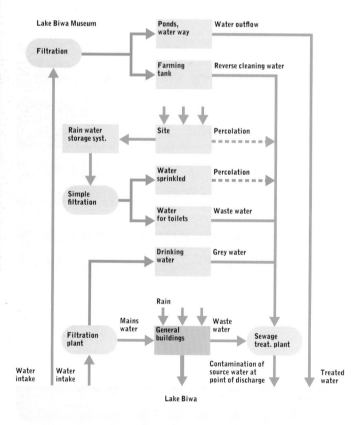

6.9

6.11

6.12 The Museum's
restaurant.
6.13 The Museum's lake
façade has a single layer of
glass in a tension mullion
structure measuring 1.5 m
wide by 9-12 m high.
6.14 Section G, detail.

6.15 External view of the
UNEP complex.
6.16 Louvred ceiling of the
Museum's interior is a stylized
'wave' design.
6.17 The entrance lobby of
the UNEP complex.

6.15

6.12

6.13

6.16

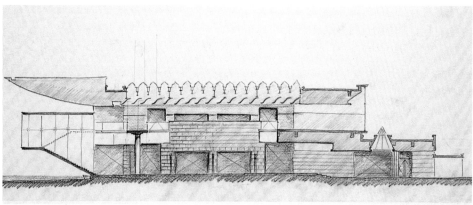

6.14

6.17

6.18 The technology and methods used in keeping the UNEP bedrooms cool in the summer.

A Air flow roof.
B Roof sprinklers.
C Natural air flow.
D Cool air.
E Air intake.
F Deciduous trees.
G Airflow path created.
H Deep eaves.

Blocking out the Heat

Deep eaves and curtains block outside heat and solar radiation. Sprinkling stored rain water on the roof draws off latent heat through evaporation. This cools areas of the roof that are exposed to the sun.

Heat Emission

Heat accumulated by the roof is quickly expelled by its airflow design. This process cools the surface and prevents heat flowing into the rooms.

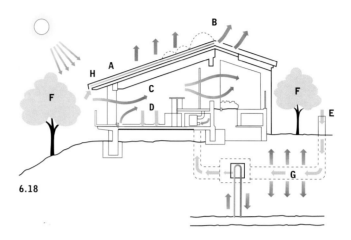

6.18

Using Natural Ventilation

At night and on relatively cool days, openings in the building allow the winds from Lake Biwa and breezes cooled by surrounding trees to enter the rooms. This natural method of ventilation and nocturnal cooling combine to produce a comfortable environment.

Cooling by Radiation

Passing cold air underneath the floor slabs cools the floor's surface. Radiation from the chilled floor gives the room a comfortable cool temperature.

Creating a Breeze

Cool air is also supplied to the rooms using two systems together. The air is first passed through the airflow path where it is cooled by losing heat to the ground and then is further cooled by groundwater.

6.19 The technology and methods used in keeping the UNEP bedrooms warm in the winter.

A Warm air.
B Floor heating.
C Deciduous trees.
D Airflow path created.

Absorbing Solar Heat

The sun penetrates the foliage of deciduous trees, passing through windows and shining deeply into the rooms.

Conserving Heat

The use of insulation and double-glazed sash windows prevents heat from escaping to the outside air.

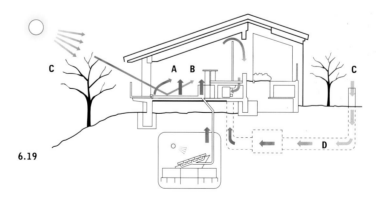

6.19

Heating by Radiation

Floor heating using water heated by the sun gives a gentle heating effect produced by heat radiation from the floor.

Warm the Breeze

Fresh outside air supplied to the rooms gains heat from the ground as it is drawn through the airflow path.

6.20 1st floor plan of Lake Biwa Museum.
6.21 2nd floor plan of Lake Biwa Museum.
6.22 South–north section of the Museum.
6.23 1st floor plan of the UNEP complex.

6.24 2nd floor plan of the UNEP complex.
6.25 North elevation of office block.
South elevation of office block.
South-west elevation of lodging block/UNEP complex.

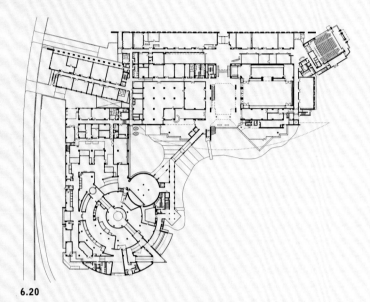

6.20

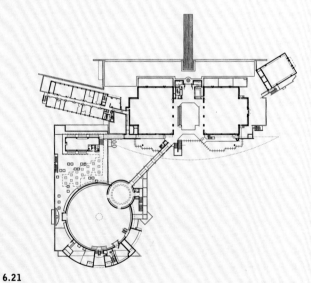

6.21

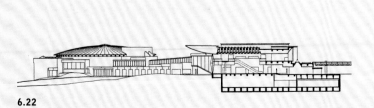

6.22

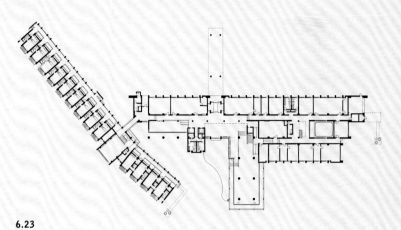

6.23

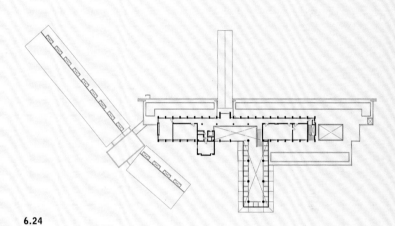

6.24

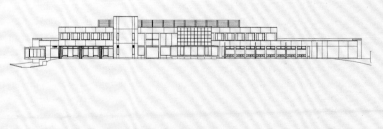

6.25

Tokyo Gas, Earth Port

Location:
Yokohama

Site area:
2,498 m²

Building area:
1,652 m²

Total floor area:
5,645 m²

Building purpose:
Office, showroom and
community centre

Number of floors:
+4, −1

Structure:
RC, SRC, S, W

Completed:
1996

7.1 A three storey glass-covered atrium forms the ecological core of Earth Port. The front glazing utilizes multiple layers of low-ε glass and the structure consists of laminated Oregon pine.

Site Features

This industrial building, Earth Port, operates as a branch office of the Tokyo Gas Company. Its design is unique in its multi-purpose functions and energy-conserving systems. As the service headquarters of a major natural gas company, it was built primarily to deliver maintenance programmes to surrounding consumers and market gas appliances. It also provides many community programmes such as nutrition and cooking classes. The building incorporates a showroom, offices, demonstration kitchens and adaptable spaces designated as teaching and/or meeting rooms. Discrete areas of the facilities are selectively programmed to preserve energy by shutting down the heating and lighting when certain staff are out on service calls.

From Symbiotic Model to Architectural Concept

The Tokyo Gas Company's conservation policies strongly promote safeguards for the environment, a comprehensive programme that has won them many awards. Earth Port's design evolved from a 'life-cycle energy-saving' plan based on a joint two-year research project with the architects of Nikken Sekkei. The result was a building model of light, airflow and human interaction, and the creation of an 'ecological core', an atrium with specific light and air attributes located along the building's length. The researchers surveyed the human use of space and how energy was allocated in modern Japanese architecture. Not surprisingly, it revealed that in modern buildings lighting and air conditioning accounted for approximately 80 % of total energy consumption. Based on their findings, the study team targeted air conditioning, lighting and conveyance technologies as areas for major reductions in energy consumption. They concluded that the maximum use of such elements as natural breezes, adaptable open spaces for human communication, and shifting patterns of daylight should have a strong presence in the building's design. Their plans would be based on one repeated, simple nucleus: the unified forces of light, airflow and human presence.

To the approaching visitor, the exterior of the building appears as a graceful, dramatic glass ark rising out of the surrounding landscape, whose atrium roof still curves against the eye at dusk when the interior is fully lit. The name, Earth Port, is very appropriate. Running east to west, the building's long-planed body sits as if gently anchored to its foundation, like a ship at rest. The four-storey structure's glass shell extends on its north façade from the roof in a dynamic motion, arching down from the fourth level to the second floor. The curved roof was designed to avoid direct sunlight penetrating the roof glass. Both north and south walls contain vast expanses of glass and the windows on the south face are mounted with light-conducting eaves. Light pervades the building from both sides, changing hourly in accordance with the sun's daily traverse around the site. A wind tower soars above the east aspect while a glass columnar addition on the west houses a stairwell. The urban zone around Earth Port has restrictions on the height of new constructions. However, despite this building's four-storey measure, its lateral body and the swell of the atrium roof give the impression of a more substantial form. Entering the building, one becomes aware of the supple rhythms created by the serpentine beams of the atrium windows and how natural light is manipulated as a visual enhancement of the environment.

Applications of the Ecological Core

The problem of earthquake-prone sites has always been a critical design challenge for Japanese architects. Most contemporary corporate buildings employ a wide range of core types, utilizing corridors, stairs, toilets, etc. as the support base, and place them within the structural elements for earthquake resistance. Frequently, aesthetics and positively-designed areas for human interaction are diluted in their intentions by the necessity of conforming to earthquake-resistant protocols. Work sites are obliged to rely on artificial light and air conditioning. Cut off from natural sunlight and airflow, these structures are massive over-consumers of fossil fuels.

7.2 External view from the
southwest.
7.3 The wind tower.
7.4 A night view of the
building from the northwest.

7.2

7.3

At Earth Port, the architectural vision sought to liberate the users of office spaces from such negative environments while still observing earthquake codes. The goal was to create an attractive space, reflective of nature, as evidenced by the small forest of trees and flowers that bloom inside the atrium; an energy-saving forum where natural breezes are exhausted via wind towers; and where human communication is facilitated by sunlit walkways and intimate seating spaces.

The Office of Wind and Light

In implementing the ecological core, the architects reinterpreted the support base, freeing it from the structure and locating it separately. This allows for daylight and natural ventilation to be distributed uniformly throughout the plant. The synergy of light, wind and people that informs the architecture is truly a contemporary expression of the traditional Japanese 'engawa' or verandah. However, here the tradition is translated into an elegant, glass-sheathed atrium open to the breeze spanning the second to the fourth floors. The ecological core is configured to achieve three major physical benefits, culminating in reduced energy consumption, human comfort and easy interaction:
• The first is utilization of natural light to the building's full advantage for lighting purpose.
• The ecological core acts a whole chimney in order to produce natural airflow.

• Both stairs and corridors are open to the atrium's core rather than being enclosed, and positioned to facilitate maximum human exchange.

Drawing in the Light

Traditionally, direct sun, despite its obvious advantages, has always posed a design challenge for architects because of its variability. The standard office building typically uses artificial light sources for both ambient and task lighting, utilizing window shades or tinted glass panes to block natural light. The architects took a contrary position, namely that the movement of natural daylight is a very desirable stimulus and makes spaces more attractive. It also allows

7.4

dramatic reductions in the energy that would
be consumed by artificial lighting.

Light is conducted from without
and dispersed within Earth Port via a series
of innovative design strategies utilizing
various types of glass technologies. The
building's exterior glass skin covers a
number of planes, allowing both the north
and south walls and the atrium roof to deliver
mass expanses of natural light. The interior
walls of the offices are floor-to-ceiling
opaque, etched glass. Luminance quality
in the building's ecological core is one
of softly diffused sun, creating appealing and
comfortable patterns throughout the
workday. The project is a state-of-the art
example of the successful use of natural

light, both as a design element and as an
energy-saving macrocosm. The designers
found that if task lighting provided at the desk
level is adequate, this would allow variation in
the ambient light environment which is more
beneficial to the human eye and to the office
worker's well-being in general. It supports
increased productivity, provides a natural
sense of time and is innately aesthetic.

Light-gathering strategies also meant
maximizing the size of the windows. The
frame in the office areas would only be
exposed to axial forces, so the width of
beams around the windows could be reduced
dramatically and the supporting columns
made more tensile and slender. This
approach to the design of the building's

exterior allowed the installation of large
windows on the north and south walls. The
depth of the office space was set at 16m to
preserve flexibility. In order to obtain a
luminosity of 300 Lux at the centre of such a
deep office space, the ceiling at its highest
perimeter was established at 3.5m.
Considerable ingenuity was required to
invent economical and safe ways of opening
such high windows within standard floor
intervals of 4.2m.

Controlling Luminance Utilizing the Hisashi
or Light Shelf

The window bays on Earth Port's south
façade were designed to uniquely pair the
traditional Japanese hisashi, a shading

7.5 How the design provides a
path for air and light.
7.6 Simulation of natural
ventilation. The chimney
effect of the ecological core
and the wind tower combine to
generate natural ventilation.
7.7 Variations of the
ecological core.

7.8 Reduction of LCCO$_2$.
7.9 The ecological core spans
the atrium from the second to
the fourth floor. The second
floor also houses the Tokyo
Gas Company showroom.

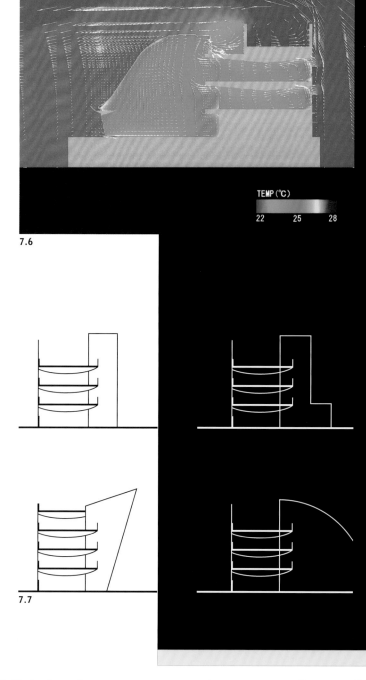

TEMP (°C)

22   25   28

7.6

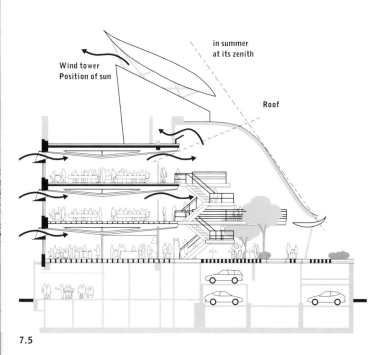

7.5

7.7

eave, with various sophisticated glass
technologies. The ceiling on this aspect of
the building slopes from 3.5m high at the
windows to 2.8m in the centre of the space.
Light shelves, 1.2m deep, were fitted above
the middle of the windows. The sun, reflecting
from the light shelf, passes through diffusion
glass on the office partitions to reach the
rooms' centre and brightens the ceiling. This
combination gives a greater subjective feeling
of brightness as well as increasing sustained
illumination within the room.

Controlled Linkage between Daylight
and Artificial Lighting

If a building is to make innovative use of
natural light and realize significant energy

saving, it's essential to implement an
advanced light-controlling technology that is
sensitive to constantly changing ambient
light. As part of the energy conservation
efforts at Earth Port, Nikken Sekkei developed
a new, light regulation system that works in
harmony with the shifting intensities of
natural light.

An overall assessment of the light
environment and luminance consumption
was a key factor in the early planning stages
of the building. The architectural team
engaged in a prediction study that would
enable them to establish daylight usage as
the primary light source for Earth Port and
maximize its function throughout the
building. Prediction of the light environment

and energy consumption was estimated
using scale models and computer
simulations. For example, the changes in
light distribution in the office spaces using
doublesided light access and light shelves
were tested. It confirmed that, compared
to single-sided light access and other factors,
a double-sided light-access system produced
far greater brightness.

On completion of the study,
measurements were taken to confirm the
findings by using a digital camera. It was
concluded that the predicted light values for
the entire building had largely been realized.
A 65% reduction in daytime energy
consumption for lighting the offices was also
confirmed.

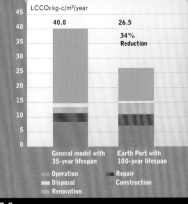

LCCO₂ kg-c/m²/year

40.0   26.5

34% Reduction

General model with 35-year lifespan

Earth Port with 100-year lifespan

- Operation
- Disposal
- Renovation
- Repair
- Construction

7.8

7.9

Utilizing Glass Technologies

The use of glass in the Earth Port project was deployed to deliver tempered daylight to multiple spaces with varying luminance requirements, and also to provide a degree of thermal conduction and insulation. Since multi-layer glass has the same insulation capacity as concrete walls, it allowed much greater freedom in the design of the building's cladding and window units. With the thermal transmission rate of the glass below 1.3 kcal/m²h degrees centigrade, any given part of the exterior of the building could be made transparent or opaque without increasing interior temperatures.

In the planning of Earth Port, the architects applied glass technologies that would suit the individuated needs of all locations. Variations were controlled by the combined use of thermal transmission and sunlight screening rates in the double-glazing of the windows. This was achieved by varying the concentration of argon gas between the panes, inserting aluminium louvres, and varying the density of metal film in Low-ε glass.

Harnessing the Sun and the Wind

Cooling and heating Earth Port presented many interesting challenges to its designers. Here was a building that had large open spaces, multiple glass surfaces and a mandate to be a shining example of environmentally-responsible architecture to the surrounding community. The installation of large size windows in the south face meant entry of abundant sunlight but with the accompanying nuisance of solar heat. The problem was solved by the light shelves that serve as a baffle against the sun and block direct solar radiation, ensuring thermal comfort even near the windows. At the same time, they give a feeling of openness and provide the office staff with an unobstructed view of the outside.

The ecological core model was intended to promote natural ventilation throughout the structure at all times. To ensure this, the architects decided to utilize the classic device of a 'wind tower'; with its stack effect, this would be an effective

7.10

7.11

method of ensuring natural airflow through-out the building, regardless of whether or not the wind was blowing. With the ecological core already utilized as a free-flowing air source, the west staircase column, which lies open to all the floors and the atrium, was used as a further wind tower. In spring and fall the natural ventilation produced by the action of these air-conducting areas maintains an even airflow and a comfortable temperature at every level of the building.

Harnessing natural resources for use in buildings means finding strategies for coping with their elemental behaviour. In some cases drawing the wind into the office spaces could dampen papers on the desktops or blow them away. For this project, repeated simulations were conducted to find window positions and opening methods which would not blow papers around. Remote control of the degree of window opening and closing was also used as a way of ensuring the ideal airflow for any conditions.

Ecological Materials

Various ecologically-viable materials were used in this project out of consideration for their aesthetic value and the need to minimize the building's lifecycle CO_2 production volume. The criteria were that they be natural, non-fluorine and recyclable, wherever possible. The range included specifically wood for beams and interior finishes, and a range of derivatives such as: exterior tiles produced from converted silt; paving stones manufactured out of waste concrete; foamed glass panels from waste glass bottles, and interior surfaces from recycled wallpaper.

Translating Traditional Architectural Features

Many design aspects of Earth Port translate traditional architectural features into new forms. Examples are:
• The engawa (verandah)
The ecological core, existing between the external and internal space, is a translation of Japan's traditional verandah.
• The hisashi (eaves)
Eaves to block direct sunlight while bringing in reflected light from ground or water is a

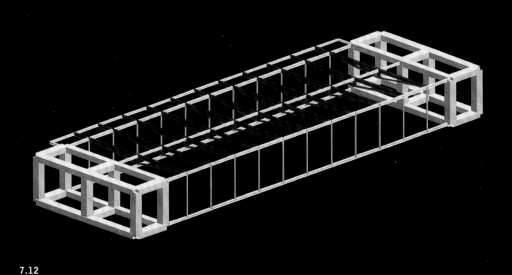

7.12

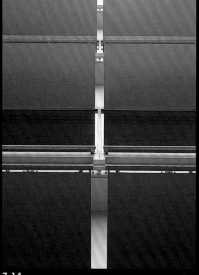

7.14

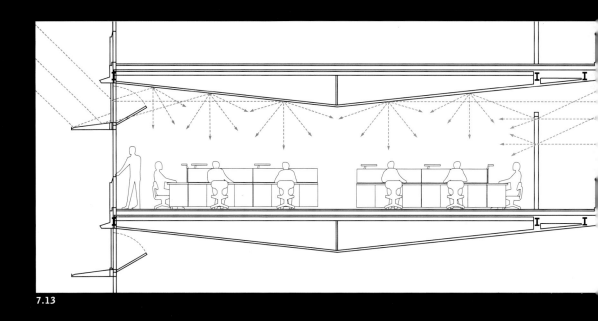

7.13

common theme in the traditional building forms of Japan and other sub-tropical areas. Deep eaves are effective at keeping out the rain, an essential function in extending the life of buildings in such regions.

• The sudare (bamboo screens)

In ancient Japanese houses bamboo screens, called 'sudare', blocked the entry of direct sunlight. They allowed privacy by preventing the interior to be visible while permitting the inhabitants to see out. At Earth Port, the concept of 'sudare' is transformed into modern materials. Aluminium louvres are sandwiched between two panes of glass, blocking the entry of sunlight while preserving the view from the interior.

• Shoji screens

Space in classic Japanese architecture was made versatile by the use of traditional room partitions known as 'shoji' screens. On the north interior walls etched glass partitions, based on the principle of shoji screens, were installed to preserve privacy in the office bays while making maximum use of the diffuse light from the north.

The Success of the Ecological Core

To test whether or not Earth Port met its environmental standards, measurements were made over an extensive period after the completion of construction. The following results were obtained showing that the building largely reached its set targets. An

investigation of the energy consumption records between April 1996 and March 1997 showed a 45% reduction in primary energy use compared to ordinary office structures. Thus Nikken Sekkei concluded that it is possible to design buildings that consume 50% less energy than the standard office block. A 35% reduction of $LCCO_2$ is one yardstick for load on the environment. All these measures yielded a reduction of $LCCO_2$ by approximately one-third compared to the output of conventional office buildings.

Earth Port was conceived as a small-scale but highly imaginative experiment in 'green' architecture. The sustained success of the project, together with its design

7.15 The glass façade of the atrium is angled at 75 degrees to ensure that no direct sunlight penetrates the building at any time of the year.

7.16 Looking up through the staircase on the east side. The treads of the stairs are constructed of grating to promote air movement.
7.17 Staircase and front entrance to Earth Port.

7.15

innovations and its commitment to energy conservation, proves that reduction of the environmental load is not a limited choice for architects, or the users of such spaces. Rather, it is a vital imperative for the future. (Architect: Kiyoshi Sakurai)

7.16

7.17

7.18 Detail of the light shelf.
7.19 Calculation of energy
saving effects.
7.20 Section detail.
7.21 Details of low-ε coated
glass.

7.18

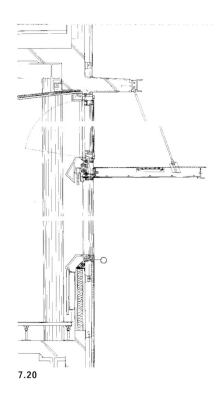

7.20

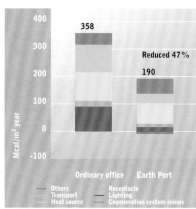

7.19

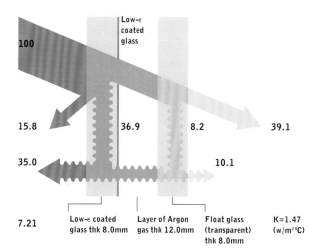

7.21   Low-ε coated   Layer of Argon   Float glass   K=1.47
            glass thk 8.0mm gas thk 12.0mm   (transparent)   (w/m²°C)
                                              thk 8.0mm

7.22 Site plan.
7.23 2nd floor plan.
7.24 4th floor plan.

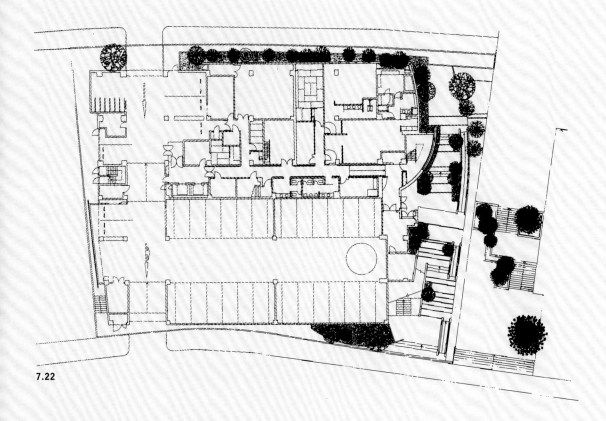

7.22

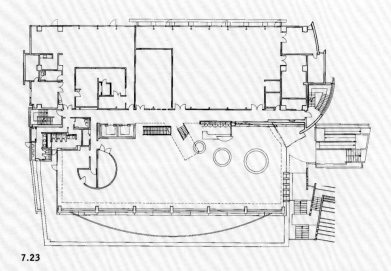

7.23

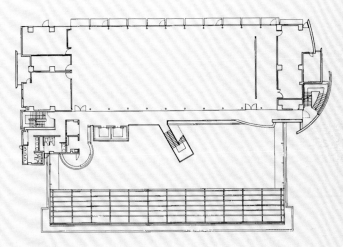

7.24

RITE Headquarters Building

Innovative
Technology for
the Earth

Location:
Kyoto

Site area:
40,274 m²

Building area:
3,449 m²

Total floor area:
6,922 m²

Building purpose:
Research centre

Number of floors:
+2

Structure:
RC, S

Completed:
1993

8.1 Aerial view of
the RITE site.

An Information Bridge between Industry and Global Preservation

The head office of the Research Institute of Innovative Technology for the Earth (RITE) is one of Japan's major 'knowledge creating' centres in a 21st century pilot community called Kansai Science City. Planned as a new park of scientific excellence, the municipality is a hub for advanced research, international exchange and the development of cutting-edge technologies. Set in the Keihanna hills, Kansai Science City extends over 154 square kilometres and encompasses areas of three cultural prefectures all steeped in the traditions of Japanese scholarly thought: the ancient citadels of Kyoto, Nara and Osaka.

RITE was established in 1990 to research technology transfers between industrial innovations and appropriate technical applications that nations need to protect the global environment. The institution, besides gathering and disseminating information, also develops technology to utilize CO_2 effectively, and researches and advances ecologically intelligent, environmentally balanced production processes. Built in accordance with such purposes, the architecture of the RITE centre had to embody the union of these ideas and be stringent in all its environmental mandates.

Nikken Sekkei's design objective for the research centre maximizes the energy resources available from the site itself,

implementing a symbiotic strategy combining soil, wind, water, natural light and trees in most areas of the facility. The location selected for the building is a hill with an elevation variable of approximately 6 m within the site. The plan encompasses two wings in an L-shaped layout with a rotunda tower set in the elbow of the main buildings. An artificial canal streams around three sides of the complex, cascading down man-made waterfalls and culminating in a pond on the north side. Most of the structure is only two floors in height, except for the rotunda, which encloses an atrium and is used as a meeting, reading and study area.

Exploiting the soil's innate thermo-dynamic properties at the site, the design

sunk half the mass of the south wing, including its western exterior walls and part of the roof, beneath the earth, from certain aspects giving it the appearance of a partially-submerged barn.

The earthen encasement is a desirable feature for this department of RITE because the wing houses several key laboratories. Much of the research conducted here includes soil bioremediation, plant genetics and gene splicing, molecular microbiology and several other areas of environmental science. The stringent temperature controls required by the lab's systems and equipment are maintained in optimum balance by the soil belt—the earth being warmer in winter and cooler in summer than exterior

temperatures. Enclosing part of the walls of the lab block significantly lowered the load on the entire air conditioning system.

Wind and Airflow

The roof of the lab block, just like an aircraft wing, is bevelled for maximum airflow capacity. This surface effectively reduces cooling loads by forming deep eaves and increasing the volume and direction of airflow for enhanced ventilation. The eaves are extensive enough to protect the laboratories from sunlight. The roof is also constructed of two layers of materials that increase the insulation performance and provide comfortable interior temperatures for labs and offices. In summer, the accumulated heat

between the two layers is expelled naturally by the wind flow along the roof created by the temperature gradient. During winter, warmed air harvested between the two layers is recirculated for heating. This ventilation method is based on chimney systems used in traditional Japanese houses. Additional airflow in the laboratories is supplied by floor-vented air conditioning. Air is propelled from the floor to the ceiling, forming a buoyant layer as it is gradually heated by thermal radiation emitted from lab workers, computers, lights and equipment. On reaching maximum buoyancy, the heat is extracted from the room via the ceiling vents. This is a highly-effective configuration for ventilation and air conditioning based on the

8.2 The research rooms.
8.3 Interior of RITE.

8.2

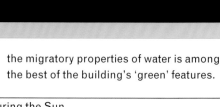

8.3

considerable speed of ascending warm air,
and provides the lab workers with an equable
and pleasant working temperature. When air
buoyancy is used for heat extraction, thermal
radiation can easily be eliminated from
any environment without resorting to more
conventional fuel-consuming methods.

Energy from the Motility of Water

RITE has a very active CO_2 Ocean
Sequestration programme, and their concern
for global water resources is reflected in
the ways water is integrated into the design
of the facility. Water circulates around the
entire site, fulfilling a number of roles at
various locations. It passes through streams,
waterfalls and pond areas to produce a

reflective and serene panorama. Beyond
its aesthetic appeal, the water is also used as
a primary agent in the building's cooling
system. The pond, stream and waterfalls
combine to form a natural cold conduit. Hot
water released from the cooling equipment
is relayed out to the pond where it is exposed
to the atmosphere. As the water gathers
speed, the heat evaporates. The stream
splashes down artificial dams and decorative
rocks as it winds through the garden. It
cascades and foams over shallow falls and is
returned to the system to be recycled for
cooling purposes.

The conserved water is also used for
a number of functions within the building.
This energy conversion method of exploiting

the migratory properties of water is among
the best of the building's 'green' features.

Capturing the Sun

Natural sunlight in the work and dwelling
environment provides a soothing and
peaceful radiance unmatched by artificial
lighting. As it changes with the passage of
the day, it evokes a range of moods in those it
touches. The shoji screens of traditional
Japanese houses produced a discrete and
malleable light that varied in response to the
hour, to the season, and to the layers of
screens that were either open or shut. Via
these simple frames, an entire house could
be open to the elements on two sides, or
selected areas closed off to let the sun

permeate through the rooms in subtle patterns.

The atrium in the building's centrepiece tower integrates the sun in a similar manner. It has a high sloped cathedral-scale roof that also serves as a solar energy 'platform'. Unique in its design, the entire surface is covered with photovoltaic cells used for both electricity and as roofing materials. The interior has shoji screens surrounding the reading room on the second floor while the tower's circular windows provide a magnificent vista of still water, manicured lawns and avenues of trees.

Trees as Building Materials and Architectural Models

More than one architect has raised the question "Why can't a building be more like a tree?" While trees present an aesthetic form and agreeable shade to human viewers, they are also a microcosm of sustainable design. A tree distils water, produces and conserves food, successfully utilizes solar energy, creates a micro-climate, produces healthy soil, biodegradable materials, is self-renewing, and provides an optimum habitat for other species. As a material, wood is fragrant and pleasant to touch. Wood is used throughout the interior of the RITE complex and is a central feature of the design.

The acreage around the site is landscaped and planted with indigenous grasses and shrubs, all at varying heights to emphasize the folds of the undulating terrain. The road to the entrance is lined with cherry trees and gardens are watered from the unified pond and stream system. The building is located strategically on its site to harmonize with the visual continuity of the surrounding countryside.
(Architect: Hisashi Yosano)

8.4 External view of RITE
and surrounding landscape.
8.5 The rainwater recycling
system.
8.6 Fountain.
8.7 Stream.
8.8 Pond.
8.9 Waterfall.

8.10 Water is a key element
in the design. It circulates
around the site, fulfilling a
number of roles. This flow
passes through the stream,
waterfall and pond to provide
a richly varied panorama to
the building.

8.6

8.8

8.7

8.9

8.4

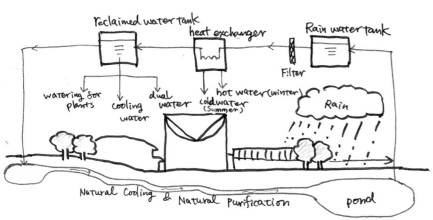

8.5

8.10

RITE Headquarters
Building

8.11 The air ventilation
system.
8.12 Floor vented air
conditioning system.
8.13 Reduction in primary air
conditioning consumption
yielded by each method.

A Solar panel.
B Laboratory.
C Machine room.
D Research room.
E Cooling tube.

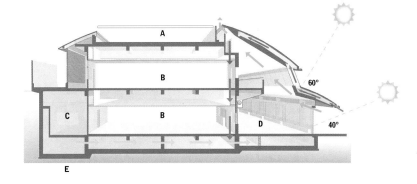

A Ventilating opening.
B Office.
C Cooling tube.

A Ventilating opening.
B Solar panel.
C Atrium.
D Cooling tube.

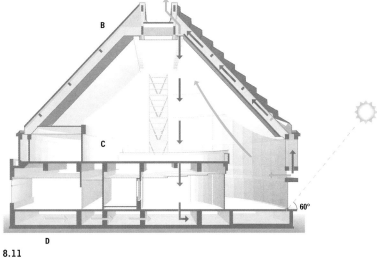

8.11

Natural ventilation (for
spring and autumn)
Airflow roof (for winter)
Cooling tube (for summer)

8.12

Original design	2281 MJ/m²/year	
Construction methods	1988 MJ/m²/year	13% reduction
Natural energy	1963 MJ/m²/year	14% reduction
Equipment systems	1620 MJ/m²/year	29% reduction

8.13

117

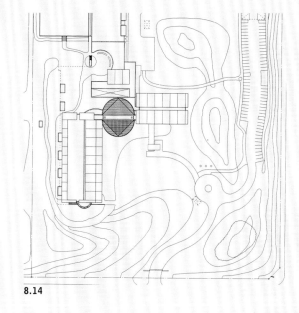
8.14 Site plan.
8.15 1st floor plan.
8.16 2nd floor plan.
8.17 South–north section.
8.18 East–west section.

8.14

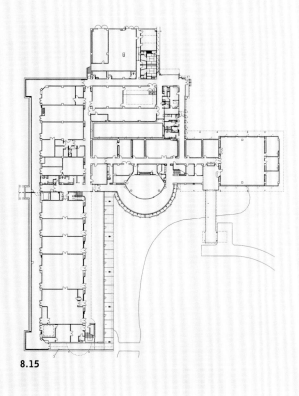

8.15

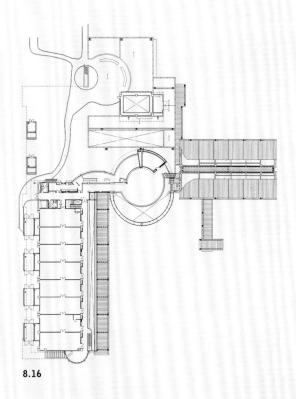

8.16

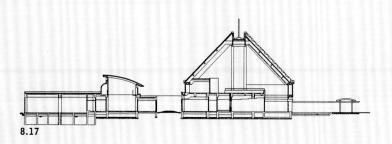

8.17

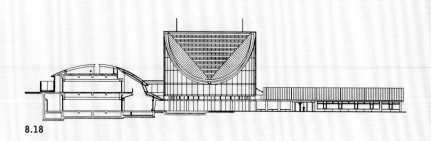

8.18

Panasonic Multimedia Centre

A city centre
building using
night cooling
with outside air

Location:
Tokyo

Site area:
13,726 m²

Building area:
7,973 m²

Total floor area:
43,926 m²

Building purpose:
Research and development
centre, with an exhibition
area and office space.

Number of floors:
+9, −1

Structure:
SRC, S

Completed:
1992

9.1 The 45 m high atrium is
the core of the building and
constructed of natural stone.

A Pyramid of Sun and Mirrors

The Panasonic Multimedia Centre is situated in a mixed section of Tokyo where the building code is part industrial and part residential. The building's commission had several key purposes, including creating a major presence for the world-renowned Matsushita Electronics Corporation in the city's downtown area. However, its main focus is to serve the locale as a multimedia R&D centre. Its design concept is based on the unanimity and fusion between the human community, nature and technology.

The site of the Panasonic Centre experiences very congested traffic flow from an adjacent trunk road on its eastern flank. Heavy local industrial production, a transitory population density and climate fluctuation all subject the immediate environment to serious levels of atmospheric pollution. These conditions created certain architectural challenges that had to be resolved in the ultimate design of the project.

The exterior mass of the building ascends from its site as a majestic trapezium of glittering steel and glass. By utilizing this form, the architects sought to minimize the effect of bulk and facilitate light access and the deceleration of wind at the base level. The core focus of the design is the rotunda atrium. Despite its immense vaulted space, the 45 m high atrium was designed as an inviting social environment where people, both visitors and staff, could relax and easily

communicate, where human activity is pleasantly supported by both natural elements and technology.

After experiencing the building's dramatic exterior, on entering the visitor is pleasantly surprised by an interior garden of natural stone and verdant plants, with a soothing waterfall fed by rainwater. The garden is a derivative of classical Japanese gardens, but here any austerity is softened by the play of water and the constantly-changing light that pervades the atrium space. The rainwater resource is retained and recycled, both for aesthetic and functional purposes. The eastern façade of the atrium is composed of a vast glass wall while the west houses the elevators and other core facilities.

An Intelligent Building with an Organic Sensibility
Given their stature as a leader on the cutting edge of the electronics industry, Matsushita wanted a highly 'intelligent' large-scale building, designed in amity with nature. They sought a holistic architecture that would reflect their own technological and environmental concerns. Three salient design solutions that evolved out of Nikken Sekkei's initial planning and were adopted in this project included:
• the 'Ireko' (or shell space concept)
• the creation of a heterogeneous indoor environment, and
• the use of natural energy systems throughout the building.

The 'Ireko' principle is a classical concept in Japanese architecture whereby space is approached by considering the layering of one environment within the other and how they are related and influence one another. This was the first time Nikken Sekkei had consciously used this idea in the environmental design of a large urban building. It could be said of 'Ireko' that the starting point begins with the human being in the core of their personal environment; from these personal areas enclosed by an ambient surround, the atrium spreads out, creating a lucid ordering of space. The impact of the form and functions of these successive spaces then extends beyond the building's envelope to adjacent, local and

urban spaces, giving those inside a sense of infinite extension to the world and the universe. 'Ireko', in its ancient context, once served to mute the threat of the natural environment and the spatial composition allowed dwellers to easily acclimatize to the outdoors. At the Panasonic Centre, nature is brought indoors and integrated into the building as an important interstice.

Creating a Heterogeneous Indoor Environment
Comfortable temperatures and bright lighting throughout buildings were once luxuries available only to royalty and nobility. However, while the arrival of artificial light and air conditioning has transformed the way human beings function in buildings, they

9.2 Site plan; 1st floor.
9.3 Aerial view.
9.4 Exterior view at night.
9.5 Details of the atrium's
interior.

9.3

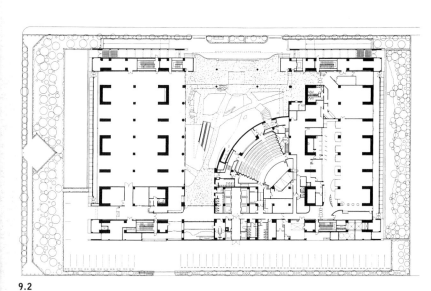

9.2

9.4

are considered a homogenizing force that dominates modern building environments. Today, there is move away from the homogeneous interior and, increasingly, designers are seeking innovative strategies that will result in highly flexible hetero-geneous spaces. This approach is vitally manifested throughout many areas of the Panasonic Centre.

The architects felt that an attractive and appropriate design should be created for each type of space, providing some preferences to users. It would also allow the user or occupant to experience nature in a highly variable semi-outdoor environment. An example of this are the office spaces arrayed on both sides of the atrium, which retain maximum flexibility, while providing comfortable, airy work spaces. The working areas allow the free intake of fresh outside air and carefully combine ambient and task-specific controls that unite natural and man-made elements.

Natural Ventilation Strategies in Large Buildings
In metropolitan areas afflicted with much noise and other urban nuisances, it is difficult to make full use of natural ventilation. Open windows can present major maintenance problems such as sudden rain, wind-borne pollutants, and in many high-rise buildings the architect faces the challenge of wind resistance. Conversely, it's increasingly essential that natural ventilation be factored into the plan, since the energy required to run major cooling equipment in many structures is a burden, both economically and environmentally. Ironically, the design of many large city buildings makes them exceptionally well suited to natural ventilation.

Because of its varied functions, the Panasonic building has high cooling requirements year round. In many areas of the facility, the thermal load due to OA equipment is projected to be as great as $100VA/m^2$. The level of energy demanded makes it the kind of facility where free cooling by outside air is a beneficial necessity. One of the design objectives was to find a way of creating controllable channels for natural ventilation within such an immense structure.

9.5

Two types of natural ventilation are used in the building. One is the normal ventilation systems that operate during daytime hours in order to maintain a suitable interior temperature for workers and visitors. If the outside air temperature is 20 degrees centigrade or below, the system can stabilize the air temperature without any need for conventional air conditioning. The other form of natural ventilation is night cooling utilizing outside air.

The plan provided openings for ventilation in the bottom of the windows on the outside walls of each floor in order to exhaust the air from the system as required. The air flowing in via the outer walls passes through a chamber under the window and into a raised floor. From there it enters the room through vents in the floor and is drawn into the atrium. Finally, it is expelled to the outside through the atrium's peak. The motivating force for this ventilation flow is a pressure differential, between the openings in the outer walls on each floor and the atrium, which is supported by the temperature gradient and the outside air speed. Fans in the floor air vents work to provide a little extra propulsion whenever the force proves insufficient.

This hybrid natural ventilation system is a Nikken Sekkei prototype that successfully combines both passive and active elements. All of the openings provided for natural ventilation have mechanisms that allow them to be opened and closed remotely as need and use dictate. A key feature of the ventilation solution is that it avoids the problem of outside noise entering the building together with the ventilation air. Instead of entering directly, the air is drawn first into the under-floor chamber where noise is baffled.

The Floor-vented Air Conditioning System
The building was expected to generate extremely high-density thermal (cooling) loads that would change position or increase frequently. This situation made it very important to install a comfortable, flexible air conditioning system that would also be cost effective. Research by the structural

9.6 Outdoor air inlets for
natural ventilation.
9.7 Ceiling and floor air
conditioning system.
9.8 Simulation of air
temperature—the effect of
the air conditioning system.

9.9 Composition of the
space wings.
9.10 Office space (floor
ventilation outlet).

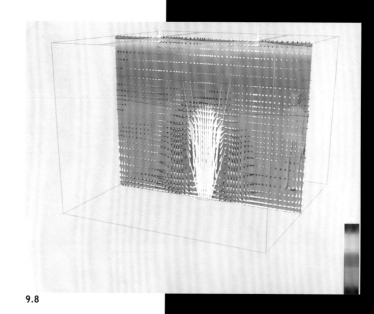

9.8

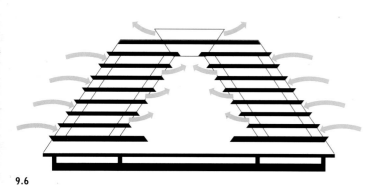

9.6

9.7

engineers led to the idea of floor-vented air conditioning. The validity of such a system was extensively tested using a variety of simulations and experiments.

Standard ceiling-vented air conditioning systems are highly inefficient for individual rooms, are difficult to adapt to changes in area division and load locations, and can prove unhealthy for office workers. At the Panasonic Centre the floor-vented system was the ideal solution to aerate and cool such a large space. The raised floor surface is used as a chamber for the passage of supply air and the fan-assisted vents blow cool air into the room. The temperature of the air delivered is maintained at the comparatively high level of

20 degrees centigrade to avoid discomfort. Return flow is drawn in through slits in the ceiling, where it passes through a chamber above the ceiling to return to the air conditioning equipment.

This kind of floor-vented air conditioning has a number of advantages. It functions perfectly as an individual air conditioning resource for people. One floor vent is allocated to each occupant and fans produce a pleasant air movement with the feeling of a natural breeze. Vents may also be arranged to integrate with furniture layout and adjusted for output air volume and temperature to suit personal preferences. The system is designed to be highly flexible and vents are easily added or relocated as

required. Cool air can be extracted from the floor chamber at any point by adding floor vents built into the free access floor. The floor outlets are supported by a pre-wiring system, so no inconvenient power supply wiring is required and the vents can be operated as soon as they are installed.

Night Cooling by Outside Air

At night, ventilation using outside air is increased to eliminate heat that has accumulated inside the building during the day. The chilled night air also cools the concrete floor slabs, which in turn act like a form of air conditioning during the day. This is an energy-saving technique that success-fully operates on the theory of cold storage.

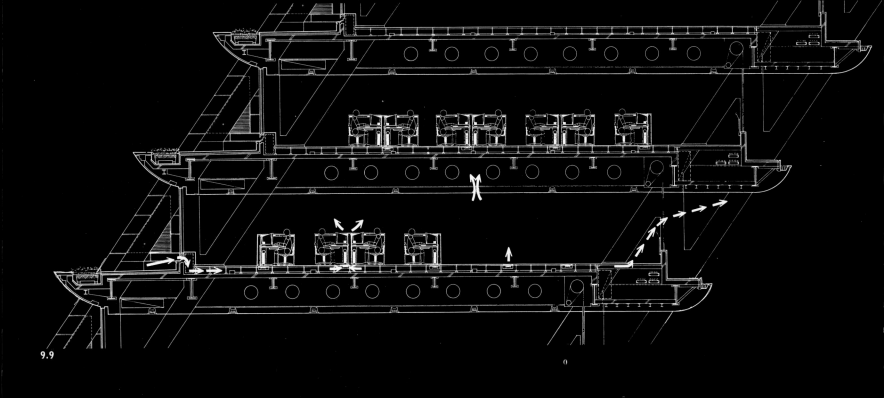

9.9

9.10

Ambient Air Conditioning for Inhabited Areas

Ambient air conditioning was planned for the outer edge of the personal space. Separate floor vents were added for the ambient air conditioning, allowing temperature adjustment in the inhabited areas of the entire space. In this case, the inhabited area is the volume to about 1.8m above the floor level. Temperatures in all occupied areas were deemed sufficient if the air was maintained at a comfortable degree for human activity.

Effective Use of Free Cooling in Local Heat Extraction

The floor-vented air conditioning system can effectively extract the heat generated within a room from people and equipment by utilizing the buoyancy created. When resulting updraughts are drawn into the ceiling without mixing them with other air and then expelled, the room-cooling load is substantially reduced, allowing highly effective air conditioning. Compared to ceiling-vented systems, this system can use free cooling by outdoor air for a much longer part of the year, achieving an energy saving factor of approximately 30%. The proven benefits of the floor-vented air conditioning system at the Panasonic Centre open up a wide range of possibilities for creating more flexible and heterogeneous environments in modern buildings.

The Fusion of Natural and Artificial Light

The atrium is a dynamic space where one can experience the attractive blending of artificial and natural light. Indeed, this sparkling interplay is a renowned design feature of immense beauty and has won its architects many honours, including the International Illumination Design Award (1994 USA). Stable diffuse solar radiation shines through the glass curtain wall on the eastern façade, creating the main light source for the entire space.

In the toplight area, transparent glass is combined with translucent glass that has an aluminium honeycomb core, and the two types of glass are arranged in an alternating pattern. This arrangement breaks up direct

9.11 Top light; black
honeycomb louvres were
installed to eliminate glare.

9.12 The light path
(direct sunlight and scattered
light).

9.11

solar radiation and scatters it to all parts of
the atrium. The sunlight playing on the
waterfall in the atrium is constantly in motion,
as if it was falling between tree branches.
Its movement across the atrium floor comple-
ments the natural texture and tonalities
of the stone garden.

In winter when the sun is low, an
array of 250mm diameter mirrors in the roof
peak reflects natural light down to the
bottom of the atrium. In the evening and in
overcast weather, fluorescent lighting
supplements the diffuse sunlight. The light
fixtures are directed upwards from the
overhanging edges of each floor on the
atrium sides, lighting the upper levels from
below. This gives an enhanced sense of

brightness and casts abundant light into the
overall space.

As the sky darkens further, accent
lighting is added and is delivered via the
450mm diameter mirrors that line the edge of
the eighth floor. The light sources are tight-
angle spotlights, which are also located on
the cantilevered eighth floor, facing upwards
for ease of maintenance. Luminance from
the spotlights reflected by the mirrors creates
a softly diffused cascade of light along the
paths and on the pool at the garden level.

This illumination method works on
many levels: it allows attractive, non-uniform
spotlighting wherever it is needed within
the ambient space, is an effective way of
enhancing the feeling of depth in the space,

and, compared to ordinary systems, it also
achieves remarkable energy savings.
These combined techniques fill the atrium
with natural light that changes with the
seasons and allows for the mirror and
spotlight systems to create equally functional
and aesthetic light patterns to illuminate
the entire space.

(Architect:Kiyoshi Sakurai)

9.12

9.13 Mirrors located along the light path reflect artificial light.
9.14 Lighting plan: mirrors reflect winter's low sunlight, creating the effect of sun filtered through foliage.
9.15 The atrium lit up at night.

9.16 Lighting design for the atrium is entirely based on reflection. Features are concealed during the day, which brings out the stream-lined beauty of the space. The system achieves easy maintenance, energy saving and is cost effective.

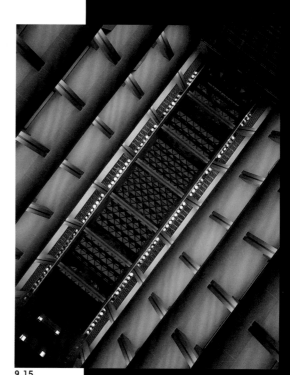

9.15

9.13

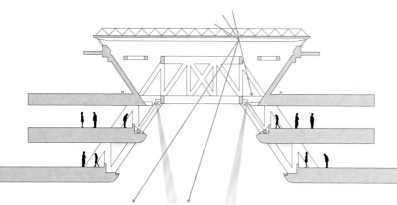

9.14

9.16

9.17 Perspective drawing of
the atrium section.
9.18 Simulation of the
thermal environment showing
vertical temperature
distribution using floor vented
air conditioning. This
demonstrates how waste heat
from office equipment rises
without becoming a thermal
load in the occupied space.

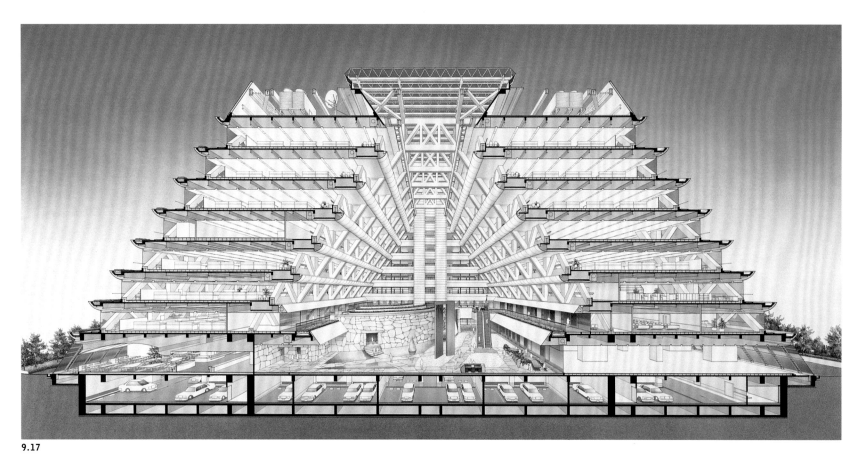

9.17

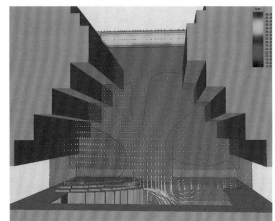

9.18

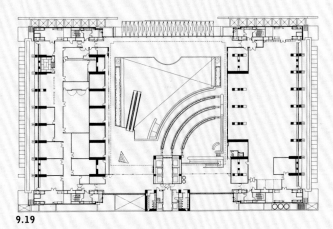

9.19

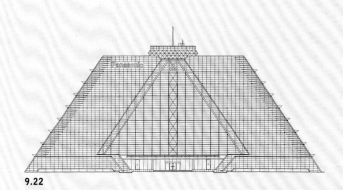

9.22

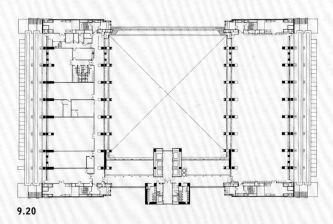

9.20

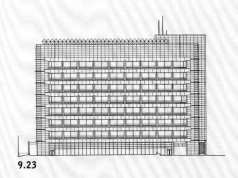

9.23

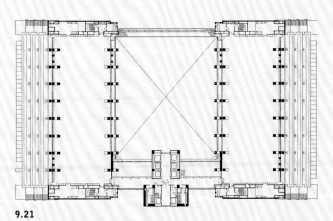

9.21

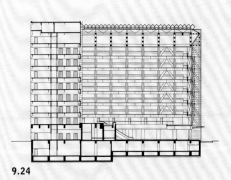

9.24

Osaka Municipal Central Gymnasium

Creating a green hill in the metropolis

Location:
Osaka

Site area:
123,986 m²

Building area:
408 m²

Total floor area:
42,664 m²

Building purpose:
Comprehensive sports centre

Number of floors:
–3

Structure:
RC

Co-architects:
Osaka City Redevelopment
and Housing Bureau

10.1 The communicating corridor on the second basement level links the main arena with the sub-arena. Circular lights are set into the reflecting pond.

Building a Sports Stadium in the City of Water

Osaka is the ancient core of the Kansai region. Situated at the mouth of the Yodo river, it has always been known as the 'City of Water'. Because of its former network of mercantile waterways, its history as a vibrant metropolis stretches back even further than the neighbouring communities of Kyoto and Nara. For 400 years it has been an energetic centre of commerce, art and liberal attitudes. Architecturally, it boasts many fine classical buildings, such as Osaka Castle built by the famous warrior, Toyotomi Hideyoshi.

As is the case with many river communities, the decline in marine transportation in modern times has led to the disappearance of important water routes and attractive urban spaces from the city's inventory of aesthetic sites. Osaka's position on the Yodo river and its historically densely-populated community has diminished the number of green spaces over time. In recent years the city's heat island effect has been growing in severity. In order to reverse this situation, the Osaka municipality has promoted intensive urban greening policies as an essential step in restoring the quality of the local environment.

A Green Landmark for the Future

The location of the Osaka Municipal Central Gymnasium is a corner of Yahataya Park in Minato-ku, close to Maijima which is the proposed venue for the 2008 Olympics. The area is a dense mix of port facilities, warehouses, small stores and residential buildings. As an urban site, it was formerly a flat plain of streets dotted with an odd assortment of architectural styles that previously left it lacking in character and distinguishing features. Now a brilliant green man-made hill ascends above its rooftops. Startlingly visible from many points, it heralds an optimistic future both for the neighbourhood and the city. The verdant emerald rise is, in reality, the cultivated roof of the Osaka Gymnasium. This comprehensive sports centre contains a main arena capable of holding an audience of 10,000, and a range of practice rooms and

administration offices. The facilities are available for official matches in many sports. The gymnasium is open to the public so the community can practise their sports such as volley ball, boxing, Budo, karate and play informal matches. Besides functioning as a sports centre, a major aim of the building is to create a stronghold of the peace that green spaces provide in the heart of the city.

The roof of the main arena is 110m in diameter and is covered with soil averaging 1m in depth. Plants and trees flourish easily on its fertile plain and the area is now considered an essential element in the city's parks system. This delightful reversal of raising nature to the roof was designed to be

symbolic of the city's commitment to preserving and revitalizing the environment.

In order to create this 'mountain' garden, the architects of Nikken Sekkei decided to sink the building 10m below the surrounding ground level. The roof of the main arena and other roof surfaces within the complex have been planted with flowers and trees to harmonize with the surrounding park areas. The main green peak is 25m tall with a pathway that traverses over its height, affording visitors access over the entire hill. Seating units in shady areas provide a magnificent vista of the city. This green landmark, like nature itself, persists in its influence on the people of the neighbourhood. For them, its leafy presence

is an encouraging landmark toward re-establishing a green vitality in the heart of Osaka.

The Structural Solution—Resistance to Massive Forces

The ground below the gymnasium site was originally full of weak alluvial deposits with a significantly high water table. Given this geological challenge, the design solution was expected to impact greatly on the costs of the major excavations required for the foundations. The first stage of construction was to build a cylindrical wall foundation 110m in diameter and 40m high. Next, the level of water inside the foundation wall was lowered, and a large volume of soil was

10.2 Site plan.
10.3 External view of the
gymnasium in its
neighbourhood setting.
10.4 Aerial view of the site.

10.5 The main arena, with a
diameter of 110m, can hold
an audience of 10,000 people.

10.3

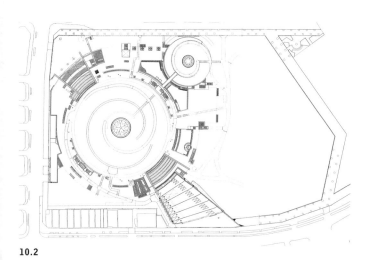
10.4

10.2

extracted. The completed earthen roof
weighs approximately 70,000 tonnes and is
110m in diameter. Supported by the strong
annular wall foundation, the weight of the
Gymnasium roof is transferred down to load-
bearing strata. The powerful buoyant force,
which pushes upwards with a pressure of
more than 10 tonnes per square metre is
reduced by extracting the water that wells up
inside the ring. This technology enabled
the use of a comparatively thin 1m mat slab.

Using the Strength and Energy of Nature
    Burying half of the building in the ground
    serves to minimize the cooling load for the
    arena. The base and sides of the building are
    also beneath street level. This allows

geothermal heat to warm the building in the
winter, while the earth's temperatures ensure
its coolness in summer. When the arena is
being used as a practice area there are no
spectators present, so the air conditioning
load is considerably low. Therefore, for
practice matches, natural light and wind are
utilized to maintain the interior environment.
These are ancillary to electrical lighting
and fuel-powered air conditioning services.
The roof's cultivated surface with its 1m thick
layer of soil and plants also acts as a
cooling mantle to restrict the entry of heat.
    If the cooling load is low, it stands to
reason that it is possible to maintain a
comfortable indoor environment using
natural ventilation alone. The engineering

and structural designs of the project enable
the use of natural ventilation for more than
half of the year, while use of the fuel-driven
cooling plant is avoided as far as possible.
To support the natural ventilation system,
air is passed through underground pits ('cool
tubes') to add the reduced soil temperatures
to the effect of the air. The air roof monitor
in the top of the arena also encourages
natural air movement.
    The ventilation rate varies with the
outside wind speed, but the system
achieves at least one air change per hour.
On completion, this will be sufficient for the
building to run on natural ventilation only
during summer and the in-between seasons.
The earth-based pits are most effective

10.5

where cooling is required. Summer sporting events act as cooling tubes for intake air, reducing reliance on the cooling plant.

As far as lighting is concerned, there is an opening of 17m in the roof over the main arena. This vent lets in daylight, providing an even illumination level of 300 lux over the whole interior during sunny days.

The Osaka Gymnasium is a successful ecological lesson in the construction of urban buildings where several considered 'green' strategies are combined to conserve energy by the use of natural ventilation and lighting. This not only reduces the burden on the environment and natural resources but also results in lowered energy costs, which represents a substantial saving in tax

revenues. Beyond these immediate benefits is the long-term impact, which in the case of this project gives the citizens of Osaka a deep sense of reclaiming their city's historic and multi-dimensional relationship with nature.
(Architect: Nobuhiro Tohmatsu)

10.6 Air is supplied to the arena through underground concrete ducts.
10.7 The gymnasium's natural ventilation system.
10.8 The interior of the membrane monitor roof.
10.9 A model of the gymnasium.

10.10 The roof of the main arena is covered with 1m of soil. Its surface area, which is 110m in diameter, is cultivated with trees and flowers bordering public pathways.

10.8

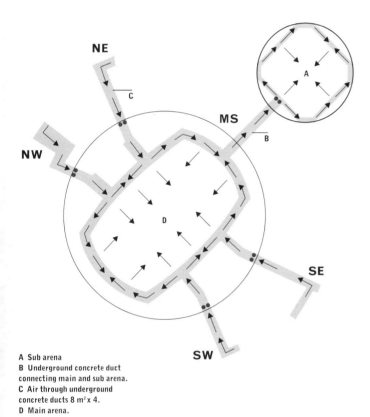

A Sub arena
B Underground concrete duct connecting main and sub arena.
C Air through underground concrete ducts 8 m² x 4.
D Main arena.

10.6

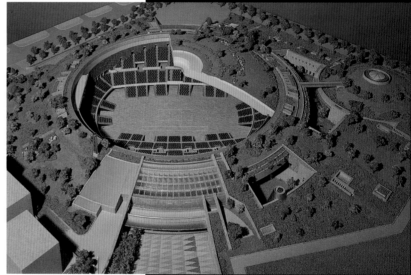

10.9

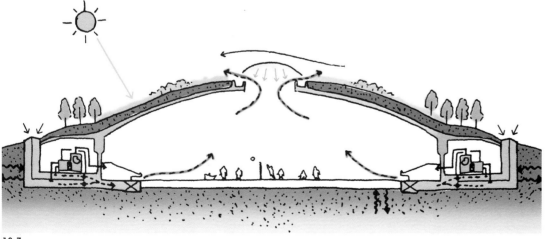

10.7

10.10

10.11 Temperatures of
three seasons.
10.12 Air supply routes
for natural ventilation.

10.13 A diagram of how the
building is ventilated in air
conditioning mode.
10.14 Record of operation
from June 1996 to May 1997.

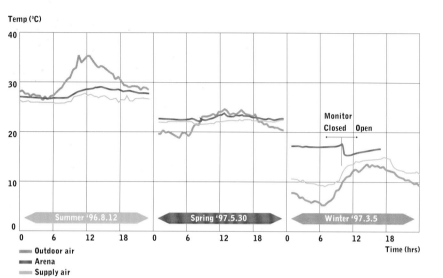

10.11

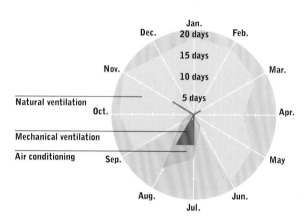

10.14

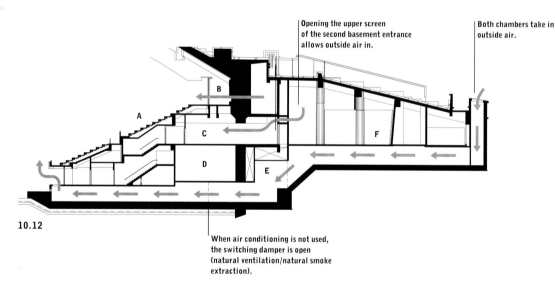

Opening the upper screen
of the second basement entrance
allows outside air in.

Both chambers take in
outside air.

A Air chamber.
B South corridor.
C South lobby.
D Air conditioning equipment
   room.
E Chamber.
F South piloti.

10.12

When air conditioning is not used,
the switching damper is open
(natural ventilation/natural smoke
extraction).

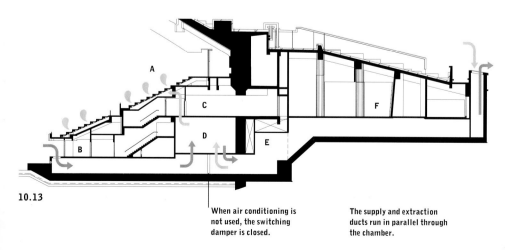

10.13

When air conditioning is
not used, the switching
damper is closed.

The supply and extraction
ducts run in parallel through
the chamber.

Air supply.
Air extraction.

10.15 2nd basement floor plan.
10.16 3rd basement floor plan.
10.17 East–west section.

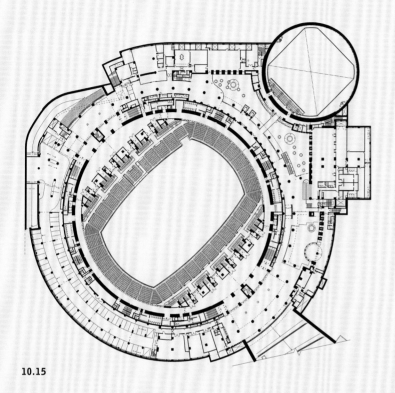

10.15

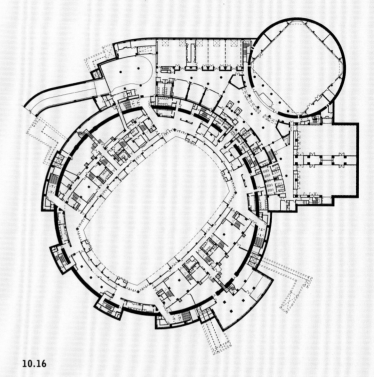

10.16

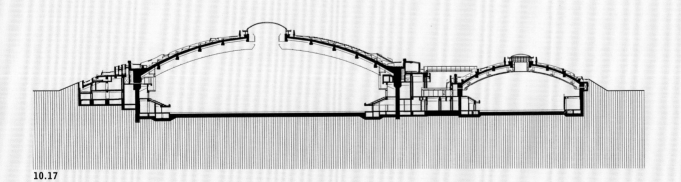

10.17

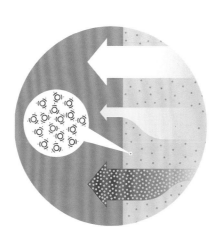

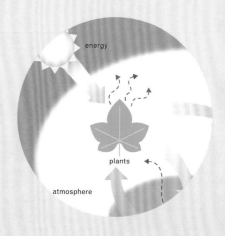

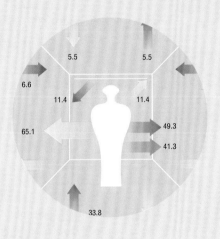

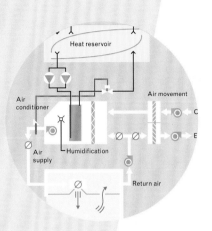

Chapter 11

Masanori Shukuya
Dr. Eng., Professor,
Faculty of
Environmental and
Information Studies,
The Graduate School
of Architecture,
Musashi Institute of
Technology

Design with Natural Potentials

The history of the built environment is inseparable from that of its time-honoured interaction with nature. Ancient human groups first created building envelopes as a defence against an environment filled with many terrors, including extremes of heat and cold, wind and rain, and the constant menace of predators. Protective shelters built by early man share a universal concept in that they sought to harness elements of natural energy such as wind, sunlight, and fire, and bring them indoors. From the archaeological remains of primal housing, it is evident that inhabitants from many cultures in the pre-historic period created rudimentary design strategies for their dwellings. These included openings—both window inlets and doors—to let in light and discharge smoke. Fire pits for cooking also provided warmth and added more luminance. Roofs became pitched or dome-shaped to ward off rain and allow air circulation. Platforms were utilized for sleeping or eating and outside shaded areas served as crude porches for social interaction. With these amenities at the command of human beings, habitats evolved to ensure a measure of comfort and security against the exterior world.

The basic architectural needs of ancient communities have bequeathed to us certain requisites for the built space, which remain constant down to the architecture of our own century even though buildings have evolved to appear quite different from pre-historic dwellings.

Most human beings are surrounded by the built environment for many hours a day throughout their lives. This 'enclosure' of daily living is fairly consistent in human history, and with primary requirements basically the same in the contemporary built environment, but with the added enhancements of the modern age. From the family house to the corporate block, buildings require efficient lighting, fresh air, and heat flow that must be well controlled so that the indoor environment will be comfortable enough for the occupants. Implementing the flow of light, air and heat through the built space is aided by many advanced innovations in building science and technology. However, this has often been at the expense of natural resources and the global environment.

Modern science and high technology has accelerated over the last one hundred years in a direction that has viewed energy and environmental resources as infinite, creating many of the biohazards that plague our world today. Contemporary architecture and building science have, regrettably, often contributed to this narrow thinking. Unfortunately, the impact of scientists, architects, and engineers in solving ecological dilemmas has thus far been limited, despite the fact that their skills hold the solutions to many of these problems. The time is long overdue to review our approach to science, technology, and architecture with regards to environmental concerns. We need to seek a new direction for architecture over the next century. This requires an essential re-alliance with nature and a permanent commitment to conservation with regard to building design. This resolution is not intended to assail technology and architecture, but rather to emphasize their very positive potentials. A shift in our attitude to design, one where nature and the environment are not degraded, will hopefully terminate our practice of borrowing irreplaceable resources from future generations.

The Mirror of Nature

The first cellular life on the earth began some 3.6 billion years ago, with the persistence of evolution constantly producing increasingly complex and highly adaptable life forms. Similarly, our present style of architectural design and building systems that dominates our environment may be regarded as an evolution from the most basic rudimentary shelters to modern urban skyscrapers.

All living systems have their ultimate predestined form within their DNA, and are programmed to grow, reproduce, and die. Communities could be considered the architectural equivalent to DNA, consisting of clients, architects, building engineers, and those who inhabit the built space. Essentially, human culture creates the programme for how buildings, villages, towns, and cities emerge, grow, and transform. Building design is strongly influenced by the societal values that predominate in any architectural time span—these same values also reflect how we view the natural world and influence its continuum. Such factors determine the programme that results. The role of architects and engineers in a well-considered building plan that works in allegiance with nature, creating better and more 'intelligent' buildings that fit future needs, cannot be underestimated.

The best way to endow a building programme with optimum sustainable functions is to observe and learn from the cohesive systems of nature itself. If we can develop an ethos and a programme that adopts and integrates the organic mechanisms of nature, then our building design will harmonize with the innate patterns of the environment. By achieving this, the idea of 'green' architecture takes on a very real and significant meaning, and is not just a hollow slogan. Adopting such an approach would infuse our cities and buildings with life-revitalizing design and architectural values that truthfully could be called 'sustaining'.

The Thermodynamic Model

It is valuable to review the realm of architecture and its associated building science in connection with biology, ecology, sociology, thermodynamics, and other influential factors, to try to create a better understanding of how 'mirroring nature' and its systems can inform our design sensibility. Thermodynamics has usually been considered as a science far outside architecture because it usually appears overly mathematical. However, if we look at thermodynamics more closely in relation to building design, we find aspects that provide us with a holistic view. There is a profound similarity between architectural function and the logic of thermodynamics, a link that furthers our understanding of nature in architecture and energy flow through buildings.

Key concepts from the thermodynamic world are exergy and entropy. Exergy is the concept that articulates 'what the resource is, and how it is consumed', and entropy defines 'what the waste is, and how it is produced and discarded'. In considering the characteristics of a building envelope system, we can assume that the system is composed of a tremendous number of particles and its right-hand side is warmer while the left-hand side is cooler. Empirical law tells us that thermal energy is transferred from 'hot' to 'cold'. The particles in the warmer side of the building envelope vibrate more strongly compared to those on the cooler side. In fact, the energy transferred as heat is a transfer of the vibration through the collection of particles that compose the building envelope system. This vibration disperses in the course of energy transfer. The amounts of energy flowing in and out are exactly the same, provided that the distribution of the temperature across the system remains unchanged. None of the energy is consumed in the course of the transfer. This is the law of energy conservation.

Under these circumstances, the energy flowing into the building envelope system is accompanied by a certain amount of exergy. The dispersal of the vibration results in energy flowing out of the building envelope system which also carries with it a diminished amount of exergy. Thus, the difference in exergy between inflow and outflow has been exhausted within the system. This is the consumption of exergy.

Next, it is important to consider how much the degree of dispersal, as a whole, within the building envelope system increases as a result of the vibration's dispersal. This is the law of entropy generation, which parallels the law of energy conservation. Fortunately, it has been proved that the amount of generated entropy is directly proportional to that of consumed exergy.

If the distribution of the temperature within the building envelope system is to be constant then the amount of entropy the building envelope system contains must also be constant. This is the concept of entropy. In a situation where a certain amount of entropy is also generated due to exergy consumption, this entropy must be discharged from the building envelope system to the outside in order for the distribution of temperature to remain unchanged. Otherwise, it turns out to be contradictory with the above mentioned characteristics of entropy contained by a substance. It is important to recognize that the energy flowing out of the building envelope system not only exits with a decreased amount of exergy but also departs with an increased amount of entropy. The building envelope system follows four steps in the exergy–entropy process: 1) the feeding on exergy; 2) the consumption of exergy; 3) the production of entropy; 4) the discarding of entropy. These steps occur sequentially and cyclically to maintain the distribution of the temperature within the system. This exergy–entropy process not only applies to a simple building envelope system, but also to more complex systems such as living organisms that eat food and consume it, thereby discharging waste into their environment. The exergy–entropy process can be configured into the planning and design of any building system, whether the space is a room, an entire house or office

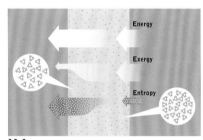

11.1

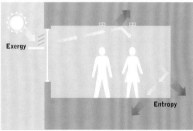

11.2a

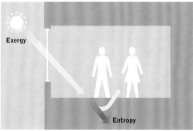

11.2b

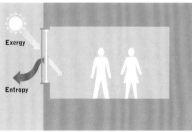

11.2c

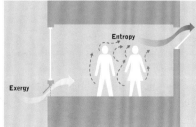

11.2d

block, a whole city and so forth. All buildings operate within the exergy-entropy process. This means that their lighting, heating and cooling systems driven by fossil fuels, electricity and other exergy sources, inevitably produce entropy, namely waste, which is eliminated into the surrounding environment.

The Passive Approach to Building Design

In designing building environmental control systems, there are two approaches: passive and active. The active concept encompasses and emphasizes the design of the mechanical systems for heating, cooling, and lighting, such as assemblies of heat pumps, boilers, fans, water pumps, ducts, pipes, wires, light bulbs and so forth. The passive or bio-climatic approach means designing systems so that various potentials found in our immediate environment are utilized creatively to provide a desired level of sustainable qualities within the built space. The adjective 'bio-climatic' describes a highly successful functionality that could be compared to the efficiency of human skin. This remarkable fascia is essential in maintaining the core temperature of the human body and is intensely responsive to variable environmental conditions. The well-conceived 'membrane' of a building operates in a similar mode, as an integration of diverse exergy-entropy processes keyed to environmental needs, both internal and external.

Many environmental problems associated with modern architecture arise when active design is totally disconnected from the passive approach. Quite a few architects and engineers appear to have forgotten what the passive mode is or, worse still, they're even unaware of the term as implying positive outcomes in building design. What is truly important is to seek the innovative integration of passive design with the active approach. Heating, cooling, and lighting systems designed from an active approach may be easily categorized as functioning within the exergy-entropy process, because they obviously feed on such resources as electricity, consume it, and then discard the waste heat. Energy systems devised by the passive design concept such as daylighting, solar heating and cooling also participate in the exergy-entropy process. The following six schematic drawings explain how exergy-entropy process functions in building systems created by the passive design approach.

a) Daylighting

Exergy derived from sunlight is consumed in the course of interior illumination. Consumption occurs when solar exergy is absorbed by the interior surfaces of the building's envelope. Thermal exergy is produced as a result of solar exergy utilized for lighting, and may also be used for space heating. The entropy generated in the course of solar exergy consumption is released into the atmosphere by ventilation or mechanical cooling.

b) Passive Heating

Passive heating strategies shift the process of solar exergy consumption from daytime to night time by designing the built space using appropriate materials that have low thermal conductivity and high thermal-exergy storage capacity. Essentially, the thermal exergy generated during daytime is banked and consumed during the night hours. Most of the entropy produced is discarded spontaneously through the building's envelope into the atmosphere.

c) Shading

An excess amount of solar exergy, namely the remaining exergy necessary for daylight illumination, is consumed before it enters the building. Thus, less entropy is generated inside the built space. This enables the mechanical cooling system to function optimally and consume less exergy in removing the entropy produced within the space. Exterior shading devices are very important in this regard, since the entropy generated within them is effectively eliminated into the atmosphere mainly by convection.

d) Ventilation Cooling

Drawing in ambient airflow through strategically located inlets utilizes the kinetic exergy of atmospheric air which is created by the exergy-entropy process of the global environmental system. Consumption of the kinetic exergy of ambient air removes the entropy produced within the built environment from such sources as the body surface of occupants, lighting fixtures, electric appliances, computer banks and others, into the near-ground atmosphere.

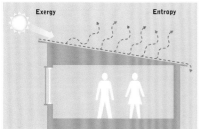

11.2e

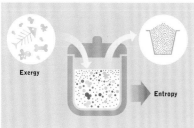

11.2f

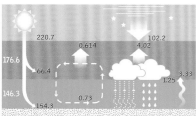

11.3a

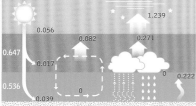

11.3b

f) Water Spraying and Evaporation

'Wet' exergy contained by water is very large compared to thermal exergy, namely 'hot' or 'cold' exergy. The consumption of 'wet' exergy decreases the 'hot' exergy generated by solar exergy consumption and can result in the production of 'cold' exergy. Methods used in building design to effect this process are roof spraying and the Japanese tradition of 'uchimizu', which involves scattering rainwater on surfaces to create a cooling effect via evaporation. The consumption of 'wet' exergy to produce 'cold' exergy or decrease 'hot' exergy is also enacted elsewhere in nature. It plays a very important role in the photosynthesis of green plants and the temperature-regulating system of the human body.

g) Composting

Microorganisms actively consume a large amount of chemical exergy contained in waste matter that is generated daily by human consumption, thereby breaking the waste material down and turning it into fertilizer. The thermal exergy produced by the consumption of chemical exergy in the decay process can be utilized to maintain the temperature inside a compost container at a desired level. This is realized by making the walls of the container thermally well insulated. The entropy produced in the process of composting is discarded within the confines of the receptacle, and eventually into the near-ground atmosphere. In all of these six systems, exergy is supplied and consumed, and hence the entropy is produced and discarded into the near-ground atmosphere.

Regarding sustainable architecture and the exergy–entropy process, designing spaces for human occupancy requires incorporating an efficient route in which exergy is rationally consumed and the resulting generated entropy is effectively eliminated into the atmosphere. This approach ensures a temperature-controlled interior comfortable enough to support and sustain human use of the built space. Therefore, this element of passive architectural design may be called 'the design of flow through buildings'.

The Global Environmental System

Our near-ground atmosphere receives all the entropy, which is produced, and discarded not only by the six systems mentioned, but also by any mechanism that involves lighting, heating, and cooling of the built environment. The near-ground atmosphere is also the repository of entropy generated and discarded by all life forms, from bacteria to plants to animals.

A significant characteristic that should be noted is that any increase of entropy contained by a substance can result in a rise in the temperature of that substance. This implies that all of the phenomena discussed here could bring about an increase in the near-ground atmospheric temperature if the surface continues to receive entropy discarded from various systems. However, what is actually occurring in nature is different; the average atmospheric temperature is almost constant from year to year, though we experience the periodic fluctuations of ambient temperature with every seasonal change. This is due to the exergy-entropy process of the atmosphere that works by feeding on and consuming solar exergy, thereby producing entropy, and finally dispersing it into the universe. We term this 'the global environmental system'.

The global environmental system receives two types of exergy: one from the sun, the other from the universe. The presence of these 'hot' and 'cold' exergy sources nurtures all life forms on the earth. The consumption of solar exergy together with the 'cold' exergy from the universe brings about the circulation of atmospheric air and water. The passive design approach for ventilation cooling described earlier uses a part of the convection air current near the ground surface, just as water spraying utilizes a part of the water circulated within the atmosphere.

All the entropy produced by climatic and biological phenomena including human beings is swept away from the near-ground atmosphere, and delivered to the upper atmosphere where it is finally eliminated into the universe by long-wave length radiation. The entropy flowing out from the higher boundary of the upper atmosphere contains all the entropy produced by activities within the atmosphere. This means that the entropy produced as a result of exergy consumption by the six systems as utilized in the passive approach to architecture is finally dispersed into the universe. The role of circulation of air and water in the atmosphere is essential in entropy disposal.

11.4 A model of an ecological
system in which plants,
animals and micro-organisms
exist symbiotically. The
exergy–entropy process is
inherent within the system.

Solar exergy is received by
plants and consumed at various
stages. The entropy generated
is ultimately discarded into the
universe via the atmosphere.

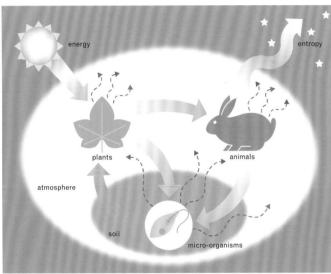

11.4

The Circulation of Matter

Our understanding of the exergy–entropy process is critical to architecture because it teaches us how important it is in the design of flow through buildings. A related phenomenon that is equally significant is 'the design of circulation'.

The importance of circulation as a design element can be investigated by making a 'thought experiment' of a heat engine and observing how it can be transformed into a sustainable technology. Imagine a model heat engine consisting of a kettle as a boiler, a pinwheel as a turbine, and a washbasin as a condenser. Some amount of water as a working fluid is kept inside the enclosed space. The water in the kettle is boiled by burning fuel and vaporized so that the pressure inside rises. Steam is propelled vigorously from the spout and makes the pinwheel rotate. The steam then flows into a part of the closed space, which is dipped into the washbasin containing the cold water. The water is released as vapour and returns to its liquid state. However, it is the flow of water from the kettle to the washbasin that makes the pinwheel rotate, but this alone cannot maintain the pinwheel's rotation. It is necessary to install a pump with a tube between the kettle and a part of the closed space dipped in the cold water. Installing a pump makes the continuous circulation of water possible as a working fluid, and enables the whole system to operate sustainably by providing a means of return, thus preventing the total dispersal of the water resource. Therefore, the presence of the pump in powering the circular flow is essential to conserve the water resource. Just as the global environmental system works between two sources of exergy, the heat engine works in similar manner—one is the burning fuel under the bottom of the kettle and the other is the washbasin containing cold water. The engine actually functions because of the combined presence of 'hot' and 'cold'. We can compare the materials used in buildings as the equivalent of the working fluid in a heat engine, and we should recognize the importance of an agent in recycling building materials which, in our sample experiment, could be regarded as the equivalent of the pump.

Conclusion

In this chapter, we have examined the passive design approach to architecture, defined as design that maximizes the use of natural potentials, which is thermodynamically rational and operates efficiently without degrading the global environment. The earth is the ultimate model of a holistic integrated designed system that has survived over centuries because of the very nature of its sustainable patterns. This dynamic organism continues to survive and maintain itself, despite detrimental human intervention and the assaults of pollution.

We are on the verge of a new century and a critical point in our history that requires us to change our direction in the way we approach nature and building design. Environmentally responsive architecture assisted by a renewed vision of thermodynamics is an important bridge in this journey. Increasingly, passive building design needs to develop new innovations in flow and circulation technologies for light, heat and air that can finally own the distinction of being called 'sustainable'.

Panasonic Multimedia Center,
Tokyo. A city center building
based on the "Ireko" concept,
(space shell concept).

Shin-ichi Tanabe
Associate Professor,
Department of
Architecture,
Waseda University

Evaluation
of Comfort and
Health in
the Built Space

Healthy Buildings

Human beings spend at least 90% of their lives inside their offices and homes. Therefore it's imperative that the interior environment serves them well by ensuring a pleasant and healthy atmosphere at all times. This is particularly essential in the daily workspace, since people are now regarded as a company's most valuable resource. Offices must be environments that attend to the physical comfort of the occupants so that their intellectual performance will be more efficient.

This requires an architecture that embraces the concept of being 'green' or 'sustainable', where the esthetic and physical characteristics of the design combine to create an enhanced environment that has excellent ventilation and low chemical emissions. Green buildings utilize natural resources in a cost-effective manner and run their energy systems without any detriment to human beings or other life forms. Consistency in the thermal environment and its air quality are important considerations in the design of green buildings. Here we discuss a human-oriented evaluation of these significant factors.

Temperature Range and Thermal Comfort

Thermal comfort is defined by ASHRAE (the American Society of Heating, Refrigeration and Air-conditioning Engineers) as that condition of mind which expresses satisfaction with the thermal environment[1], meaning one which is acceptable to at least 80% of the occupants of a given space. Generally, in this topic's field of research, the narrow definition of optimum thermal levels is negative, in that building users should not feel any thermal discomfort at all.

Conversely, there is a positive condition of perceived thermal satisfaction. Comfort that includes changes over time in natural phenomena often produces very attractive built spaces. However, the stimulus created by change is not always necessarily agreeable to every occupant. Application must be adapted to the type of space concerned. One must also consider that the occupants of a building will differ widely in age, activity, dress style, and will generate other mitigating conditions.

Six Important Factors in the Thermal Environment

Humans maintain thermal equilibrium through shedding most of the heat generated by their bodies out to their surroundings. Influences that govern this process of heat exchange between the body and its ambient space are termed the 'thermal environmental factors'. These main determinants, which impact on the perceived thermal comfort of the human body, are a) metabolic rates, b) clothing, c) air temperature, d) radiant temperature, e) airflow, f) and humidity. The unit for measuring the human metabolic rate is described as a 'met'. A single met equals $58.2W/M^2$, defined as the rate of metabolism for a person sitting quietly. Clerical work raises the rate to 1.1–1.2 met. The degree of insulation of a subject's clothing is expressed in 'clos'. One clo is $0.155 M^2/W$ (Figure 12.1).

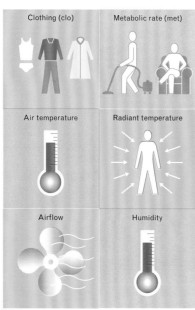

Clothing (clo) | Metabolic rate (met)
Air temperature | Radiant temperature
Airflow | Humidity

12.1

PMV (Predicted Mean Vote)

The PMV or Predicted Mean Vote theory, proposed by P.O. Fanger of Denmark, is a hypothesis that estimates perceived heat levels using the six factors[2]. To attain thermal neutrality, there must be thermal equilibrium, also the subject's average skin temperature and evaporative heat loss must be within certain suitable ranges. In the comfort equation, the average skin temperature and evaporative heat loss are taken as factors of metabolic rate. Therefore, the thermal equilibrium equation is expressed in terms of the six factors alone. In 1984 this approach was internationally standardized under ISO-7730.[3]

By substituting in the six factors the thermal sensation that would be felt by a large majority of subjects under those conditions, and giving the perceived temperature a numerical expression, Fanger proposed a relationship between the PMV (Predicted Mean Vote) and the PPD (Predicted Percentage of Dissatisfied), as shown in figure 12.2. Under ISO-7730 the recommended comfort ranges of values of PMV and PPD were -0.5<PMV<+0.5 and PPD<10%.

SET* (Standard Effective Temperature)

SET* (or ET* - Effective Temperature*) are perceived temperatures based on a theory by Gagge et al.[4] To distinguish it from the old, empirical effective temperature rating known as ET, the new version is called 'Standard Effective

12.2

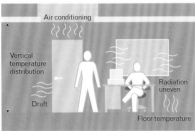

12.3

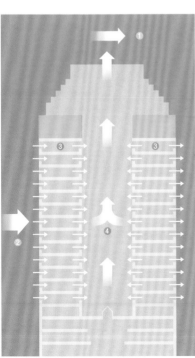

12.4

Temperature', (or ET*), and is based on the mean skin temperature plus the wetness of the subject's skin. However, skin wetness (w) and mean skin temperature (ts) is not simple to estimate. To make the calculation easier, a physiologically controlled two-node model was used, dividing the human body between 'core' and 'shell' elements. The Standard Effective Temperature (SET*) is defined as a typical state where the subject is seated at rest, wearing 0.6 clo in calm air of average radiant temperature equals air temperature. Under the SET*, clothing is modified by metabolic rate, with a standard amount of clothing specified for each metabolic level. This method allows the thermal sensation and comfort levels at different metabolic rates to be evaluated. It's also applicable in evaluating hot and cold environments, including the comfort range. There is no major difference between the assessed values provided by SET and PMV close to the comfort range.

The ASHRAE Comfortable Room Temperature Range

Thermal comfort is generally expressed in terms of thermal environment indices such as PMV, but sometimes it is difficult to understand the situation from the values themselves. If a number of thermal environment factors are set as constants, the comfort range can be expressed in terms of the operating temperature. For example, let's assume it's a summer day with a wind speed of 0.1 m/s, the average radiant temperature equals the air temperature, and the other conditions are 0.5 clo, 1.2 met and 60% rh, therefore the comfort temperature range is 23–26. In winter, with 1.0 clo, 1.2 met and 40% rh, the comfort range is 20–24. The seasonal difference in comfort temperature attributes is the difference in clothing. ASHRAE 55–92 rating indicates the comfort temperature ranges assumed for winter and summer. These ranges imply suitable clothing worn for ordinary office work both in winter and summer, and in calm air. This largely agrees with the ASHRAE thermal environment standard of 55–92, which is a PMV range of +/-0.5.

In Japan, subjects tested for temperature perception in an artificial environment chamber produced neutral temperature values (figure.12.2). When we compared these readings with subjects tested from the USA, Denmark and Singapore, we found that there was little difference between races in the temperature perceived under neutral conditions.[5] However, there are a number of arguments about the upper limit of relative humidity.

Local Discomfort and Fluctuation

Despite situations where the overall perception of heat and cold is neutral, radiant asymmetry, drafts, vertical temperature differences and floor temperature can still produce localized thermal discomfort. Where these problems exist, the overall interior climate can hardly be described as thermally comfortable. The primary requirements for benign thermal levels are; a) environmental conditions that are within the thermally neutral range; b) and local discomfort within the acceptable range (figure 12.3).

Fluctuation and Nature

It could be unhealthy for the human body to be exposed to an environment of uniform temperature and humidity. The natural environment fluctuates constantly and such fluctuations have an important impact on survival and behavior. (These variables serve as bio-chrono stimuli, and are influential in the growth and reproductive periodicity of many life forms.) Recent innovations in sustainable architecture, with regard to the environment, have sought to create transitional semi-outdoor spaces within buildings that draw in natural variations. Airflow is one example of a fluctuating element that can be manipulated with positive results for the built space. Clearly there are qualitative differences between natural and artificial air movements. Wind also has its own flow patterns and directional harmonies. In experiments on subjects simulating a summer day without air conditioning, air movement varying in strength with a sinusoidal rhythm was perceived as more cooling.[6] Recent data indicates that an office building using natural ventilation, such as the one in figure 12.4, provided a wider comfort range of temperature than one utilizing only air conditioning and where the windows were sealed.[7] Occupant satisfaction and comfort expectations in spaces where natural fluctuations and rhythms are incorporated are becoming a new theme in relation to energy saving design.

12.5 Various types of
under floor air conditioning
systems.
12.5a Underfloor diffuser
system.
12.5b Underfloor diffuser
system and heat exhaust
partition.
12.5c Underfloor Diffuser
system and personal HVAC
system.

12.6 The mobile
measurement cart (TESSA).
12.7 A computer image
of travellers at Kansai
International Airport
illustrating predicted skin
temperatures of human
subjects, both stationary
and mobile, in the thermal
environment.

12.5a   12.5b   12.5c

12.6

12.7

Personalization and Satisfaction

Personal control over the environment is an important factor in occupant satisfaction. However, this does not mean that they are always in absolute charge of their ambient environment. Rather, people are satisfied with the conditions that they can control. Besides air conditioning, the same is also true of other elements, such as windows that may be opened. Air conditioning can easily be designed for personal preference through the use of floor-vented or ceiling-vented air conditioning.[8]

Methods of Evaluating Thermal Environments
The Thermal Mannequin

In evaluating thermal environments, a method is required that can ascertain sensory quantities through simple and objective measurements. This has led to the use of the thermal mannequin to avoid the work of developing trial-and-error experiments repeated on human subjects.[9] A model with a skin surface heat-emission element is used because of its excellent response time. The artificial body has control and measurement functions built into each of its 16 segments (figure 12.5).

The Mobile Measurement Cart

The mobile measurement cart (TESSA) was developed to perform detailed calculations of the thermal environment of spaces and occupied spaces that are not usually measured.[10] (figure 12.6). It is also used for boundary conditions in evaluating environmental body temperature regulation models. In the past it was regarded as common sense to measure for a long period at a fixed point, but the TESSA method makes it possible to take detailed measurements around the occupied area from each point. After 10 to15 minutes the cart can move on to the next area to be measured.

A Numerical Model for Calculation of Body Temperature Regulation in 65 Segments

Our research group developed a numerical calculation model for body temperature regulation that divided the body into 65 segments.[11] The aims were environmental evaluation incorporating the human subject's history of temperature exposure, and evaluation of spaces with temperature distribution. This model is used in the assessment of atrium and semi-outdoor spaces through which the subjects move. Each section is divided into four layers: core, muscle, fat and skin. In order to solve the thermal equilibrium equation for human beings we need to know the following for each body section. Heat capacity and heat production, the convection heat exchange with the blood, heat exchange via conduction, the evaporative heat exchange, and the sensible heat exchange at the skin's surface. However, these values are not constants in the human body and are altered by many environmental factors. Therefore, these values are calculated at intervals by solving the body temperature regulation model. The deviations of each part from the set temperature are converted to sensor signals and the perspiration, blood flow and heat generated by shivering, which are the control results, are calculated (figure 12.7).

The Indoor Atmospheric Environment

The atmospheric pollutants that pose a threat to people's health continue to accumulate annually. However, the menace of chemicals found inside buildings is also a grave problem. Chemicals are the major suspects in most cases of sick building syndrome and are accountable for many work days lost due to illness. The list of hazardous chemicals found in the work space specifically includes formaldehyde, VOCs (volatile organic compounds), wood preservatives, plasticizers, anti-termite treatments, insecticides and agricultural organo-phosphorus compounds.[12] In new office buildings chemicals are emitted from construction materials, fixtures such as furniture and carpets, printed matter, cosmetics, cleaning agents, office equipment and other sources. Total VOC (TVOC) is an index of atmospheric pollution. TVOC values of 3 mg/m³ fall under Level I, which has a low level of impact. Level II, at m³ or above, has a high likelihood of some impact.[13]

Ventilation Efficiency

It is very difficult to reduce the emission of pollutants to zero both for interiors and the urban environment. Therefore an appropriate amount of

12.8 Indoor atmospheric
pollutants.
12.9 Measurement by FLEC
of the volume of chemicals
emitted from building walls.

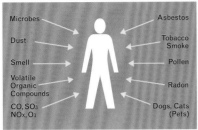

12.8

12.9

ventilation in the built space is required. In Japan, in most cases, ventilation is based on CO_2 demand control, but in the future further consideration will have to be given to ventilation for the removal of pollutants generated from the indoor space. Even where ventilation volume is the same, displacement air conditioning, which provides a high proportion of fresh outside air, is increasingly favoured. Floor-vented air conditioning systems can also be displacement air conditioning systems. Fully mixed air conditioning units require measures to prevent short-circuiting. Systems can be evaluated using concepts such as ventilation efficiency and the age of the air. Measurements are made by using a tracer gas, or by calculation.[14] Compared to full mixing, occupants are able to obtain a flow of fresh, outside air, even if the ventilation volume is fixed (figure.12.8).

Evaluation of the Volume of Chemicals Emitted by Building Materials

Another effective method of reducing the concentrations of chemical pollutants in buildings is to reduce the amounts emitted from construction materials (figure.12.9). This approach requires measurement of emission levels from a range of different materials utilizing such technology as a FLEC (15) machine or ADPAC system. The chamber method is used to measure the amounts emitted. ASTM and ECA reports discuss small test chambers in detail. In Europe the size of small chambers is 50–1,000l. Of course, pollution from chemical emissions is not just a symptom of new buildings. The problem is

also produced during the demolition and disposal of older buildings. These dilemmas show how increasingly important it is for architects and engineers to find a fundamental philosophy and methods for designing with recyclable materials.

Conclusion

The preservation of human comfort and health is an integral part of the concept of green buildings, and also of the science and research that informs their architecture. A comfortable building should be achieved with the lowest possible burden on users of the space, with the design incorporating sustainable benefits for their immediate community, the natural world and, ultimately, the global environment.

Shuzo Murakami
Professor,
Institute of Industrial
Science,
University of Tokyo

Analysis of Flow,
Temperature and
Diffusion Fields:
From Human Scale
to Urban Scale

Airflow and the Environment

Airflow is deeply linked to the quality of the environment in which we live. It controls the wind's impact on buildings, ventilation performance, and the distribution and movement of atmospheric pollutants. With today's mounting concern for the environment, it is expected that an increasing number of architects in the immediate future will apply airflow analysis to the planning of buildings and towns. In reviewing environmental dilemmas and new progress made in methods of analyzing flow fields, temperature fields and diffusion fields, we find it's now possible to link together all the physical phenomena which shape our environment and analyze them as a whole. This process is due to the remarkable advances made in numerical simulation techniques built around Computational Fluid Dynamics (CFD).

In general, airflow is given mathematical expression in terms of air convection and diffusion phenomena. However, the physical components involved in the formation of flow, temperature and diffusion fields include air heat transport, radiation (and also solar radiation), material and moisture transport, and heat conduction. The environmental problems facing us can be viewed as complex phenomena created by the composite linkages of these elements in various time and spatial scales. Coupled simulation makes it possible to perform structured investigation into these complexities. This method provides a platform from which we can analyze the effects of measures taken to improve the environment in buildings and cities. Figure 13.10 illustrates the conceptual form of one such coupled analysis.

This chapter surveys recent developments in the analysis of flow, temperature, and diffusion fields, from flow around the human body to flow on a regional scale, and summarizes how this increasingly important technology plays a critical role in the development of sustainable architecture with regard to environmental concerns.

Advances in Techniques for the Analysis of Airflow

Previous methods of analyzing airflow, particularly in the construction industry, were based on measurements made from models of interiors or from on-site observation. We benefit from the great progress achieved by research into experimental methods, such as effective correlation to scale model experiments. The wind tunnel is now the standard tool for model tests and it is widely used in construction to measure airflow around buildings, and to make it visible. Other traditional devices for measuring air speed are the Pitot tube, the hot wire anemometer and the thermister anemometer. They are still widely used, despite the fact that the ultrasonic anemometer was invented around 20 years ago. However, all these measuring devices are located within the airflow, frequently creating a problem for the researcher. The body of the device itself obstructs airflow, causing slight disturbances that can lead to errors.

In recent years, non-contact anemometers such as the LDV (Laser Doppler Anemometer) have come into use. This advance has yielded a great improvement in the precise measurement of turbulent phenomena. The greatest progress in various measurement technologies is the arrival of digital technology that allows us to collect and process data automatically. Prior to this, the handling of long-term and continuous data had reached its limits, in terms of both sheer volume and the processing time involved. The advances in high-speed computers and digital technology in the second half of this century has totally transformed the methods used for analysis of flow fields, temperature fields and diffusion fields. It's now possible to gather and process such information very rapidly and the analysis based on the data is much more reliable.

Modern airflow analysis utilizes both numerical simulation technology of CFD and CG (Computer Graphics) technology. Turbulent flow models developed for CFD, such as the k-e type dual equation model and the LES (Large Eddy Simulation) have recently been introduced into the building industry and applied to non-isothermal flow fields and diffusion fields. The results gained are being used to further enhance turbulent flow models for the analysis of the complex flow fields, temperature fields and diffusion fields during heating and cooling.

The diffusion of CG technology is highly significant and invaluable in architectural design. The flow of a fluid (in this case air) generally can not be seen with the naked eye, but computer graphics can easily render the distribution of air speed, temperature, and concentration in a space, making them clearly visible. This allows the architect to plan interior spaces with much

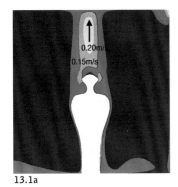

13.1a

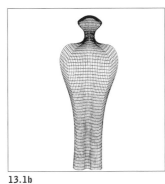

13.1b

13.2a

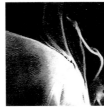

13.2b

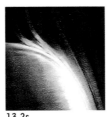

13.2c

more immediacy and accuracy. For the kind of construction where there is high output of a single product, the ability to virtually experience aspects such as flow fields, temperature fields and diffusion fields in advance is an enormously important tool in building design.

Analysis of Flow Fields, Temperature Fields and Diffusion Fields around the Human Body

Human beings generate metabolic heat in direct proportion to the degree of body activity, forming a buoyant airflow around them. These flows are often stronger than we perceive them to be. Figures 13.1a and 1b present the results of an analysis of the flow field around a person standing at rest in a still indoor space. Maximum air speed just above the head was observed to reach approximately 23cm/s. This number has been confirmed in experiments using thermal mannequins and real human subjects.

Figures 13.2a, 2b and 2c display graphic depictions of airflow around the shoulder in a real human subject, a thermal mannequin and a CFD analysis. All the results are very close to each other. The movement of heat between the inner areas and the surface of the human body has recently been incorporated in the Gagge two-node model, making it possible to use coupled simulations for detailed analysis of the exchanges of heat between the body and its surroundings. Figure 13.3b displays a type diagram of an analysis and figure 13.3a illustrates the exchanges of heat between the human body and the indoor surroundings, as produced by the analysis. These results predict the warmth or coldness that will be perceived by the human subject, and can assist in making the indoor environment comfortable.

Analysis of Flow, Temperature and Diffusion Fields in a Room

Before the widespread use of CFD, the analysis of flow, temperature and diffusion fields focused on the most obvious airflow sources in a room, such as air conditioning vents and passage of the wind through the space. In most cases, these subjects were chosen for analysis. Otherwise, the space would be taken as a uniform whole for the purpose of analysis, as with definitions of the number of ventilation air changes. If it was necessary to examine the distribution of air speed and temperature in a space, experiments were usually conducted on scale models. Figure 13.4 shows an experiment on a 1/20 scale model of a Tokyo sports stadium.

The rise of CFD completely changed the established methods of investigation and research, making it quick and easy to perform detailed analyses of the three-dimensional structures of flow, temperature and diffusion fields (figures 13.5a, b and c). It also allowed researchers to couple radiation, convection, heat conduction and even heat load calculations with these analyses. In figure 13.6 we can see the results of a predictive analysis with summer temperature distribution in an atrium during cooling.

Coupled simulation using CFD has provided techniques for the solution of complex phenomena, such as the detailed analysis of a subject's perceptions of heat and cold, and an analysis of ventilation rates. Such analyses, which were not possible by older methods, are now available for use in environmental planning. Figure 13.7 illustrates the results of a LES-based analysis of air age in the diffusion field from a vented airflow. Air age is defined as the length of time air stays in a room after entry without being vented out. The marker colour corresponds to the age of the air.

Analysis of Flow, Temperature and Diffusion Fields Around Buildings

Research into airflow around buildings was originally considered a prosaic subject mainly concerned with wind pressure coefficients that are the environmental conditions required in calculating ventilation and air passage. This situation changed radically in the late 1960s when urban building trends gravitated to the design of very tall buildings that resulted in problems with wind and impact. These dilemmas stimulated research into airflow around buildings to the point where the subject took its place in architecture and construction engineering as an important discipline. Figure 13.8 is a photograph of a wind tunnel experiment that visually reveals the effect of wind around a super-high-rise building originally planned for the Ikebukuro district of Tokyo. In recent years, research has extended its investigations to the diffusion of pollutants around buildings, with regard to atmospheric pollution in their immediate vicinity and the location of their ventilation intakes.

13.3a Heat balance between
the human body and
surrounding walls. Red arrows
indicate heat transfer by
convection, yellow equals
radiation and blue the total
evaporative heat from the
skin.

13.3b Heat exchange between
the human body and the
surrounding environment.
13.4 Experiment being
conducted on a 1/20 scale
model of a Tokyo sports
stadium.

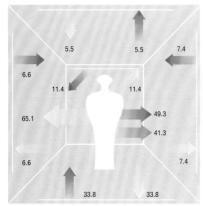

13.3a

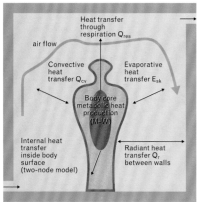

13.3b

13.4

Formerly, research in this field was mainly conducted in wind tunnels, but this method has been improved upon by the increased use of CFD. In figure 13.9 we can clearly observe an instantaneous flow trace around a square column, as predicted by LES.

An important new development in exterior airflow around buildings that commands great attention is research into the analysis of the thermal environment in outdoor spaces. Figure 13.10 displays a conceptual diagram of this research. Based on CFD, convection, radiation, moisture transport and other factors are related and analyzed. This makes it possible to investigate the effects of planting and other ecological strategies around buildings that assist our coexistence with the environment. At the same time, systems used for evaluating the interior thermal environment are called upon to assess exterior thermal environments as well (figures 13.11a,b,c and d).

Analysis of Flow, Temperature and Diffusion Fields on a Regional Scale

Research into airflow on a regional scale is a growing field applied to winds at sea, over land and locally in mountain ranges. More recently, CFD-based numerical analysis methods have been developed for weather forecasting and great advances are being made into the study of winds over selected regions using this technology. Further investigations are under way using a numerical model called the 'urban climate model', to gain a comprehensive understanding of the mechanisms which shape our urban weather conditions.

This model couples and analyzes the transport of air, heat, moisture, the radiation and conduction of heat through the ground. Figure 13.12 is a conceptual diagram of the urban climate model. The model is being developed further and subjected to analysis by simulations that include phase variables such as cloud formation, and chemical changes, including atmospheric pollutants such as generated oxidants (figure 13.13).

Analysis of the urban climate using numerical models is one of the largest and most detailed applications of CFD. Using this method it's possible, for example, to compare the urban environment of Tokyo today with that of the city in the Edo period. This technology will soon enable researchers to predict changes in the urban climate as a result of future urban development. The inclusion of this application in urban planning will provide architects with a powerful tool for studying the effects of planned measures to improve and protect the natural environment.

153

13.5a View of a large atrium space.
13.5b Velocity vector distribution of the same atrium space (cooling case without rooftop ventilation).
13.5c Temperature distribution in the atrium (cooling case without rooftop ventilation).

13.6 Comparison of predicted and measured results for vertical distribution during cooling in summer.
13.7 A non-isothermal flow field in a room predicted by numerical simulation.

Markers are coloured according to the age of the air. Blue equals young, green denotes middle and red equals old.
13.8 Wind tunnel experiment to visualise the effect of wind around a super-high-rise building.

13.5a

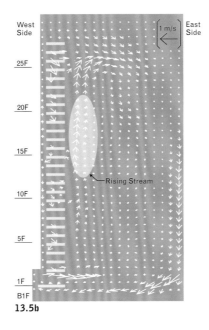

13.5b

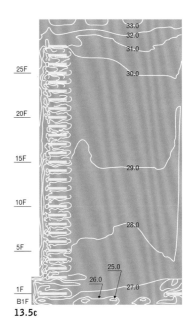

13.5c

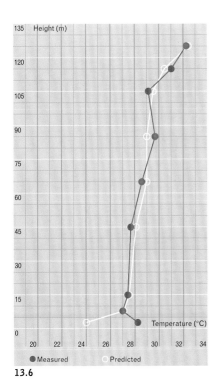

13.6

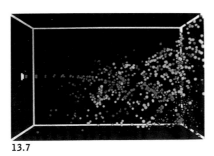

13.7

13.8

13.9 Path lines across
the prism of a square cylinder.
13.10 Physical phenomena
and transport and heat
equations used in coupled
analysis in environmental
regulation of an outdoor space.

Key to 13.10
1 Air temperature equation:
Navier Stokes equation.
2 Heat transport equation.
3 Contaminant transport
equation.
4 Water vapour transport
equation.

5 Radiant quantity transport
equation (long and short wave
lengths).
6 Heat transmission equation
for heat in the walls and
ground.
7 Heat transfer balance
equation in human models.

13.11a Analysis of the
outside thermal environment
in summer (by modified k-ε
model). Velocity vector.
13.11b Analysis of the
outside thermal environment
in summer (by modified
k-ε model). Horizontal dis-

tribution of air temperature
at the height of 3 metres.
13.11c Analysis of the
outside thermal environment
in summer (by modified
k-ε model). Horizontal distribution of SET* (Standard
Effective Temperature).

13.11d Conditions of
analysis: a case representative
of Tokyo at 3:00pm from
a height of 74.6 metres with
the wind (3.0m/s) from the
south and the sun's altitude at
45.2 degrees.

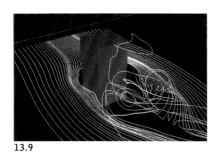

13.9

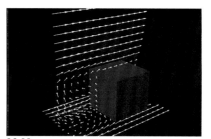

13.11a

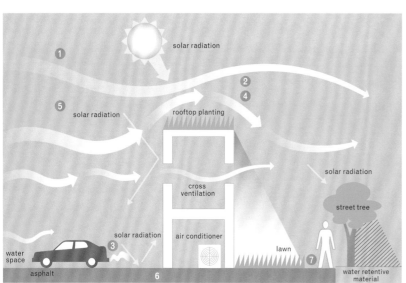

13.10

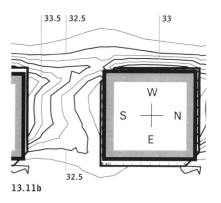

13.11b

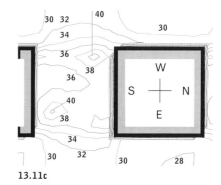

13.11c

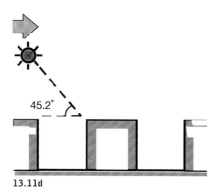

13.11d

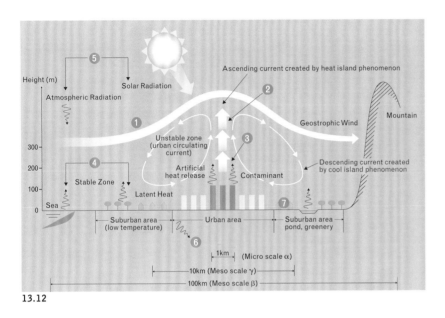

13.12

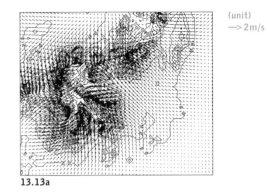

(unit)
—> 2m/s

13.13a

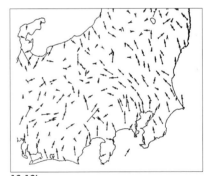

(unit)
5m/s —>
2m/s —>

13.13b

Chapter 14

Akira Hoyano
Professor,
The Graduate School,
Tokyo Institute of
Technology

Analysis of
the Urban
Environment
using Remote
Sensing

The Urban Environment as a Microcosm of Global Environmental Problems

The functions and complexities of cities traditionally offer such benefits as artistic and cultural concentrations, business facilities, educational centres, and a communications infrastructure. Over 60% of the world's people now live in urban areas and their communities continue to expand. Unfortunately, pollution and other biohazards also tend to accumulate in cities. A burgeoning population of major consumers and certain artificial aspects of modern life frequently overwhelm remaining green belts within the urban landscape. Continuing deterioration of city environments contributes heavily to the destruction of the world's ecological systems, and is counter-productive to their social and economic value. Thus, the problems of the urban environment are a true microcosm of environmental afflictions happening on a global scale.

The range of environmental detriments generated by cities is considerable (figure 14.1). The seven most common forms of pollution found in urban sites are atmospheric, water, soil, noise, vibration, ground subsidence and foul odours. These seven are designated in the Japanese Basic Law for Environmental Pollution Control. Other polluting factors reported are waste products, electromagnetic wave pollution, obstruction of air movement and direct sunlight. Beyond these menaces, humanity and other life forms also have to contend with the broad-area problem of the heat island effect. Such violations of the planet we depend upon are the results of man's actions. Ozone depletion, acid rain, global warming and other ecological transgressions are all universally recognized as being linked to the urban environment. Since many of these detriments are complex and densely interwoven, it's difficult to quantify their relationships, either temporally or spatially. Therefore, monitoring and forecasting the quality of the urban environment from the global perspective is increasingly important.

Buildings, the External Space and the City

Wherever humanity exists, the environment is affected by their impact. Even a small house on a deserted prairie creates a new climate around it, just by its presence alone. This effect is multiplied in urban centres. Cities encompass a great number of built-up areas that enclose many spaces corralled by buildings (which we call 'the exterior built environment'). Each of these confines forms its own special microclimate. Every microclimate, by its area effect, then becomes a building block for the macro-scale urban climate. The micro-scale directly regulates the indoor climate. In the past, building science tended to focus on the design and construction of individual buildings and the creation of their comfortable interiors, without much knowledge or consideration of the microclimate. However, we now know that the exterior built environment has a central role in the formation of a comfortable and livable urban setting, and influences the built space, both inside and out. As living environments, indoor spaces, the exterior built environment, urban centres and the globe itself, all influence each other.

The major dilemmas of urbanization are changes in land use and land coverage, increased energy consumption and the relentless discharge of pollutants. But what exactly are the relationships between these issues and urban microclimates that interact closely with the lives of citizens, the broader urban climate, and the formation of extensive climatic phenomena? Such questions necessitate quantitative prediction methods that enable us to easily and quickly gauge the state of the urban environment. Architects and building engineers need accurate tools to quantify and identify problems in order to propose specific solutions to create cities that co-exist in unanimity with nature.

Quantifying the Urban Environment

Today, city planners and architects involved in regional expansion and urban redevelopment require and expect detailed preliminary evaluations of how buildings will impact on the environment. Such informed perceptions on the physical state of cities and their existing buildings are essential for minimizing ecological detriments in future building programmes. Accurate prediction, evaluation and monitoring of the urban environment require the construction of an efficient information-gathering system utilizing appropriate technologies. Cities are shifting the emphasis from the pursuit of comfort in their building agendas to a greater concern for the environment. In such settings where

14.1 Environmental problems in cities and remote sensing .
14.2 A nocturnal image of the earth as observed by the Defense Meteorological Satellite Programs (DMSP).

Clusters of lights are a combination of illumination from buildings, transport networks, streetlights and other sources.

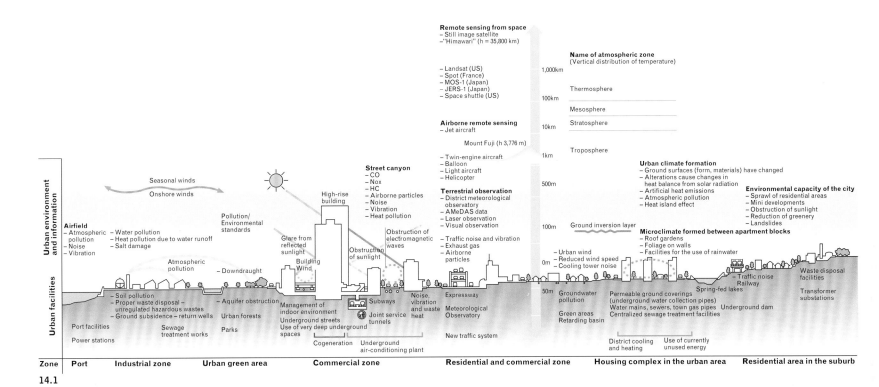

14.1

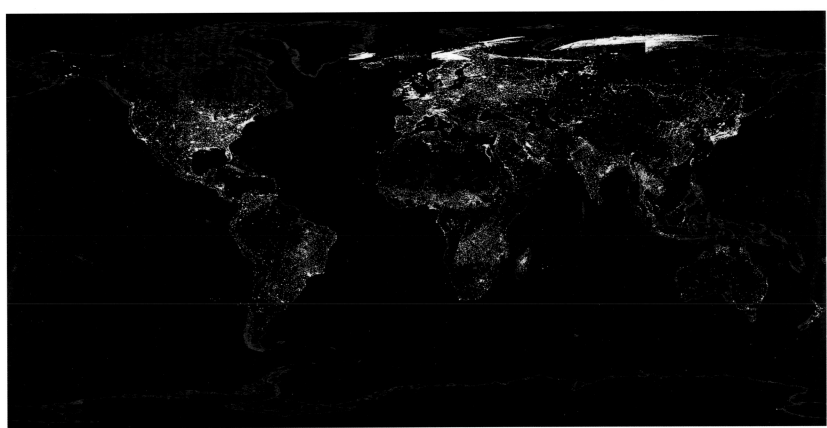

14.2

14.3 Two different applications of composite colour
images of using multi-
spectral data. The original
image is taken at Fukuoka,
Japan, from 1,500 ft height,
11:27 am in July.

14.3a Blue: visible band
(0.49-0.53 μ Green: visible
band (0.49-0.53 μ), Red :
near infra-red band (0.76-
0.80 μ)
14.3b Blue: visible band,
Green: near infra-red band,
Red:Thermal infra-red band.

14.3a

14.3b

change is swift and vigorous, the methods employed for collecting relevant data must be rapid and easily reproducible. This kind of evaluation requires the gathering of diverse and wide-ranging information on the urban environment, in addition to archived data previously acquired by city planners and civic governments.

A Return to the Ecopolis

The assessment of environmental impact also involves reflecting on the kind of urban development pursued in the past, which put efficiency first. However, changing attitudes, driven by the decline of the urban environment, now point to an increasing regard for cities whose architecture harmonizes with nature. Such municipalities focus on the climatic characteristics of the region and the natural potential of its land, without any detriment to the human community and other life forms, and can be called Ecocities or the Ecopolis. (This title evokes the classical concept of the city where design frequently incorporated a formalized but revered interpretation of nature.)

The development and renovation of city areas calls for the comprehensive measurement of environmental information, starting with the distribution of vegetation and permeable surfaces. Another important task for evaluating the comfort of the urban landscape is to ascertain and monitor the state of the environment, with reference to the heat island effect and other hazards. In these situations the application of remote sensing is an invaluable and important technology, because it can operate simultaneously over a wide area without any contact or interference with its subjects.

The Capabilities of Remote Sensing

Remote sensing is really a general term that encompasses several scientific techniques which sense and record information from subjects at a distance. However, the current form of remote sensing that has stirred much interest is more narrowly defined. This is 'the use of sensors mounted in satellites or aircraft to measure the spectral strength of electromagnetic radiation emitted or reflected by objects on the ground, and use the of those spectral characteristics to remotely distinguish the condition or nature of the subject'. The process measures, collates, analyzes and evaluates collected data.

Cities as seen from Space

Figure 14.2 is a composite satellite image assembled from cloudless views rather than a single picture. It depicts the night side of the globe taken from space, using remote sensing. In addition to light, such as the visible aurora of the North Pole, wildfires, and field burning over Southeast Asia and Africa, there is startling brightness from cities spread across North America, Europe and Japan. The entire Japanese archipelago is so brightly lit that its outline is almost completely visible from space. This image demonstrates the enormous amount of energy consumed by lighting from streets, buildings, and vehicles. If we take these bright regions to be cities and assess what proportion of the earth's surface they cover, even within the 30% of the globe that is land, the result would be very small. Nevertheless, they clearly have great impact on the world's environment because of their high-energy consumption and the output of toxic emissions.

At any one time, a considerable portion of the earth's surface is covered by clouds and obscured from the view. Such weather patterns make information-gathering procedures in the visible and infra-red wavelengths impossible. However, Synthetic Aperture Radar (SAR), an imaging technology that uses microwaves, is currently attracting great interest because it allows remote sensing in all weather conditions.

The hardware for remote sensing from space has already advanced through several generations and progress in the field is rapid. The ground level resolution of generally available satellite data is now down to a few tens of metres, but that is scarcely adequate resolution for the detailed examination of cities. However, the advent of commercial satellite sensing, which rivals remote sensing by aircraft, will provide data with a ground resolution of a few metres. Such data could be used in the examination of urban sites for preparing all-important ground coverage maps, as well as for monitoring the urban environment and compiling environmental databases.

14.4a   14.4b   14.4c

Mult-spectral imaging

Another increasingly popular area of remote sensing is multi-spectral imaging. Within the spectrum of electromagnetic radiation, only a very narrow range of wavelength, 0.4–0.7 m is visible to the human eye. By contrast, multi-spectral scanners mounted in satellites or aircraft can, as the name implies, provide images in a number of spectra, from visible light to the thermal infra-red ranges. A subject on the ground produces characteristic values in each wavelength band. Therefore, the superposition of data in three wavelength bands can give a more comprehensive picture of the state of the urban environment. Figure 14.3a represents the data for two wavelengths in the visible bands, in near infra-red it appears as blue, green and red respectively. In this image, trees, grass and plants appear red. The reading clearly reveals their distribution and vitality plus many other aspects of vegetation cover in the city. Figure 14.3b shows the visible near infra-red and thermal infra-red as blue, green and red respectively. In the daytime it's possible to read the absorption and emission of heat from the ground surface.

This technique can render information about the reflection of sunlight and the distribution of surface temperature simultaneously. White areas have intense sunlight reflection and high surface temperatures. Black shows the reverse. Shadowed areas and water surfaces appear as black. High surface temperature sites show up in red. The red sectors are mainly those where the ground is covered with artificial materials, such as sport grounds, paved roads and building rooftops. Locations covered with plants appear green because their reflection of daylight is large only in the infra-red range.

This kind of visual representation clearly shows that zones with dense concentrations of housing give very different readings from fields and forests. Even within residential areas, these images illustrate the contrasts between the arrangement of buildings and cladding materials. These characteristics can be used in statistical methods to analyze the features of land usage in a city, and in the preparation of land coverage maps.

International deliberation on global problems that are city-related requires detailed information, which allows worldwide comparisons on a common basis. We can expect the use of environmental monitoring by remote sensing to increase. Its wide-ranging, simultaneous and cyclical properties make it well suited for swift appraisals of rapidly expanding cities in developing countries, and the examination, beyond national borders, of environmental damage from acid rain and other similar issues.

Urban Heat Islands

The record of urban development to date has heavily emphasized function and efficiency over environmental quality. Sadly, it's rare to find any positive directions made toward the urban climate in the recent history of many cities. Rather, the cost of maintaining a comfortable indoor environment has become the ecological burden of future generations. However, remote sensing has made the unseen thermal environment of cities visible, allowing clear documentation of its condition, whether healthy or polluted.

Let us examine a remote sensing image recorded on a clear summer day from an aircraft over the centre and suburbs of Sendai, a city of one million people that's surrounded by lush forests. Figure 14.4a shows vegetation coverage produced by using a type of MSS image in an automatic classification method. One can clearly see the city's sprawl extending into the forests and rice paddies. Figure 14.4b is a map of vegetation coverage derived from the same kind of multi-spectral image by an automatic classification method. One pixel is equivalent to 10m x 10m on the ground. Black pixels represent an area that excludes all vegetation within the pixel.

Information about the ground surface temperature in the area can be seen in figure 14.4c which is a thermal image showing temperatures in coded colours. If we compare this image to the vegetation distribution map, we find that sites that hold abundant water, such as the sea, forests and rice-paddies, have surface temperatures more or less the same as the air temperature. The built-up centre of Sendai and the highly developed residential sectors around the city are covered with artificial materials and have almost no vegetation. These locations exhibit the highest temperatures, and the outlying suburbs are also far hotter than the adjacent wilderness and rice paddies. Sendai is known, ironically, as a city of forests, yet there is very little vegetation in the city's centre

14.5a

14.5b

14.5c

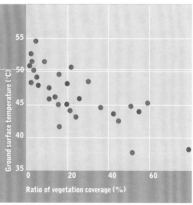

14.6

and residential belt. Wherever greenery and surface water have been eliminated, the surface temperature soars above the air temperature by 20 °C or more. Such a condition, ecologically speaking, could be defined as an urban desert. Heat density in cities is often derived from many man-made sources and is not just defined by air temperature alone. Heat radiation from the ground surface is a major factor in the formation of air temperature and contributes substantially to intolerable heat levels in urban environments.

The relationship between average surface temperature and vegetation coverage rate is a ratio of many districts (figure 14.5). The numbers for the average surface temperature were calculated from remote sensing images taken in clear, daytime weather during summer for areas with a range of ground coverage conditions. Results showed that wherever the vegetation coverage falls below 30%, those areas begin to exhibit high surface temperatures. Some districts with almost no green canopy can reach temperatures as high as 55°C. Even at night, the road surfaces, due to prolonged exposure to the sun during the day, hold their temperature at nearly 40°C. Such environments, with their oppressive retained heat volume, undermine the comfort and health of their residents, both human and animal. There is little chance of being refreshed by a cool evening breeze. The inhabitants are more likely to sweat from the radiant temperatures.

A Thermal View of a Pleasant and Interesting Urban Environment

Imagine an attractive modern city landscape—a scene that conveys the immediate impression of a prosperous and thriving community in a pleasant and refreshing environment. However, the sky, which could be described as a giant source of heat and cold, can hardly be seen from inside the deep canyons formed by the high-rise apartments and office blocks. Road surfaces soak up the sun's heat during the day and never cool further than the air temperature. The city's centre, built of similar contemporary materials, presents a barren concrete vista devoid of grass, trees, and other vegetation (figure 14.6).

The quality of the exterior built environment is defined by the design of buildings, the ground surface, and the extent to which the natural world is a presence as part of the whole. Effects, such as those described above, result from the thermal environment. They are not only determined by the spatial forms used in the planning of cities and buildings, but also the kind of building materials utilized.

Figures 14.5a, 14.5b and 14.5c are thermal images taken from the Sunshine 60 building in Ikebukuro, Tokyo, over a night and day in summer. On examining the pictures together, the effect of the Gokokuji forest in the centre of the image is prominent. In areas of wooden or concrete buildings, the temperature pattern is reversed between day and night. We're mainly looking at the rooftops of wooden houses and the walls of concrete buildings, but the difference between their heat capacities is very obvious. The road surfaces and concrete structures, that absorbed solar energy during the day, release it to the atmosphere throughout the night and into the next morning. This pattern reinforces the phenomenon of 'tropical nights', where the air temperature remains abnormally high. If Japan's summer heat island effect is to be alleviated, there must be a fusion with greenery in which roads and concrete buildings, all carrying a high heat capacity, will be veiled by plants, preventing direct sunlight from reaching them.

However, in a questionable policy of disaster prevention, demolition projects are now underway in many regions where there are dense concentrations of wooden buildings to reduce their vulnerability to fire. Despite the confirmation of iron clad data, cities, where the heat island phenomenon is already severely pronounced, stubbornly persist in destroying wooden architecture to fill their streets with more modern steel-reinforced concrete buildings. Narrow lanes that once afforded a degree of shade are being eliminated and opened out for use as car parks. There is an irony in making cities safe from fire by tearing down wooden buildings and exposing the residents to intense heat saturation. Without any sustainable considerations in their building plan and a place for nature, such communities are in danger of becoming urban 'furnaces' where everyday life is rendered unhealthy and insufferable by oppressive and abnormal air temperatures.

Veiling Buildings with Plants

Cultivating green areas in Japanese urban areas, as a means of raising the

14.7 Surface temperature
distribution for a city in
the early morning on a clear
summer day produced by
heat balance simulation.
The commercial zone (right),
where concrete buildings are
clustered, show high heat
capacity and heat retention.
In contrast, the residential
area comprised of wooden
buildings (top left) show
a considerable decrease in
temperature.

14.7a, 14.7b Surface
temperature distribution
for an entire city produced by
heat balance simulation.
Red: reinforced concrete
buildings.
Yellow: wooden buildings.
Black: paved with concrete.
Gray: paved with concrete.
Brown: bare earth.
Green: grass.
Dark green: trees.

14.7a

14.7b

quality of a city's environment and comfort, calls for an increase in planned parks, gardens and planted sectors that keep pace with expanding building programmes and an increasing population. Considering the wider environment of most regions of the country, there should be no contradiction between development and planting. However, in a country rich with vegetation such as Japan, urban growth is accompanied, to a greater or lesser extent, by major deforestation. This practice is particularly severe in hilly suburban residential locations. Therefore it is vital to consider how much of the existing vegetation can be conserved to ensure the quality of the environment, rather than depending on replanting programmes that take can decades to renew deforested areas.

Thus, the position of planting within developing urban areas depends on the climatic characteristics of the region. In an age where most cities have evolved to become extremely artificial environments, there is now a renewed awareness of the environmental-regulating effects of vegetation. Wherever 'greening' programmes are promoted as a strategy to raise the standards of city living, landscaping conceived to work in a positive alliance with architecture in improving the environment becomes an imperative. This means using plants in an effective way and in a manner that also brings an aesthetic quality to the outdoor space. 'Urban development veiled with vegetation' is an approach to building cities that will treat the earth gently and minimize disruption to its ecological systems. The creation of a city that harmonizes with nature is the keystone of the Ecopolis.

Towards the Prediction and Evaluation of the Urban Environment

We've reviewed the value of remote sensing in acquiring and assessing important data on the urban environment and its applications in city planning, and also the benefits and methods of greening areas to produce better cities. However, our task has only just begun. We need to combat the increasing degeneration of the thermal environment that is so evident in Japan because of the country's low latitude. The heat island effect and other similar effects in our climate plus the growing number of microclimates are causing a grave deterioration of the urban living sites. These detriments are further aggravated by the heavy consumption of energy for cooling air. There is also a strong relationship of their effects, both directly and indirectly, to global warming and ozone depletion.

Prediction of surface temperature distribution, which largely controls the thermal environment of built-up areas, allows evaluation of the thermal environment of living spaces and helps build databases for city microclimates and urban climatic simulations. Such assessments begin with the infinitesimal. Figure 14.7a show an example of the micro-scale approach: a 1/2500 scale simulation of surface temperature distribution for an entire city area based on key urban planning and vegetation-distribution maps. Simulation of this kind involves a multitude of parameters involving light, heat, air temperature, humidity, water and the state of ground coverage in order to discern their concentrations. Data must also be gathered on the intensities of air conditioning energy consumption, heat generated by lighting, automobile heat emissions, water vapour, pollutants and other factors that contribute to surface temperature dispersal.

Any debate on how to build optimum cities must include specific strategies for their design and planning backed by quantitative environmental forecasting techniques. Such measures need to begin at the micro level. From this point, the basic elements that compose the larger environment and the forces that shape the urban milieu, can serve as the input conditions, and continue seamlessly on to the macro scale. The data generated by forecasting technology reveals on many levels just how much cities impact on their surroundings and the global environment, and are rapidly becoming a valuable tool to the practice of sustainable architecture.

Chapter 15

Yoh Matsuo
Professor,
Meiji University,
Professor Emeritus,
The University
of Tokyo

Techniques for the Thermal Analysis of Buildings

The Advance of Thermal Analysis

The greatest single development characterizing transformations in buildings over the last fifty years is the advent of air conditioning technology. It differs from the passive, localized adjustment methods used in the past, in that it attempts to produce a comfortable thermal environment for occupants in the entire indoor space. Moderating interior temperatures by air conditioning could be described as a very American design concept. However, with the growth of the Japanese economy and the raised expectations of living standards, this method of cooling our homes and offices has become an essential element of the built space. The popularity of air conditioning in Japan also exists for more practical reasons. The country lies in the Asian monsoon belt and suffers from extremely humid heat in the summer and too many of our buildings are tightly sealed structures composed of heat-retaining steel, glass and concrete.

The function of air conditioning equipment, at least in its ideal form, is to bring temperatures throughout the total indoor space under thermal control. Therefore, at the design stage investigative techniques are required to conduct a detailed analysis and evaluation of the thermal behaviour of the whole building. In 1967, Mitalas and Stephenson published the 'Response Factor' algorithm as a means of conducting this kind of inquiry. (Software applications on the method first appeared in the 1970s.) Another example of analytical procedure published by the Society of Heating, Air Conditioning and Sanitary Engineering of Japan, was the 'Dynamic Thermal Load Analysis Program; HASP/ACLD/1973'.

In the late 1970s, particular attention was given to air conditioning as the largest consumer of energy in buildings, thus creating a widespread demand for energy-saving design in architecture. Concurrently, there was a growing awareness that design could also reduce energy use in the building, particularly the external wall. These exigencies instituted and motivated the development of thermal analysis techniques. The Energy Conservation Law (The Law concerning Rational Use of Energy) was enacted in the same period. It included standard values known as PAL or Perimeter Annual Load for energy-saving performance in building shells that were derived from the results of dynamic analysis.

The 1990s brought a new worldwide urgency to the tasks of environmental conservation and sustainability. Out of a number of major initiatives developed and promoted to halt environmental degradation, the reduction of CO_2 emission through energy saving in the operation of buildings, and particularly in the adjustment of the thermal environment, continues to be of prime importance.

The significance of the role of building thermal analysis has increased over time, to the point where it's now considered an indispensable tool for the design of buildings and air conditioning equipment with high energy-saving performance. The rapid rate of urban development, the advent of new buildings materials and technologies, and advances in architecture has created an expanding demand for such research and assessment. In order to keep pace with extensive building programmes in many urban centres, thermal analysis has evolved its methods to become a more detailed and accurate predictive tool.

The Building as a Heat Conduction System

Detailed thermal analysis requires calculation of the state of heat conduction throughout the fabric of the building at each moment. This kind of calculation is made possible by the response factor algorithm mentioned earlier. However, the thermal state in indoor spaces is strongly influenced by the geographical location of the building, and the activities that take place inside it. Mere knowledge of only the physical fabric of the structure is insufficient. What we must analyze is the response of the indoor space to thermal excitation received from both the exterior and the interior of the building.

The subjects of a comprehensive analysis, including this kind of excitation, can be arranged as follows:

a) Climate – Climatic conditions of the region – External thermal excitation – Meteorological data

b) Building – Building thermal conduction properties – Thermal response system – Thermal analysis code

c) Activity – What is done inside the building – Internal thermal excitation – Heat generation patterns.

In short, there is the climate outside the building and activity inside it. The

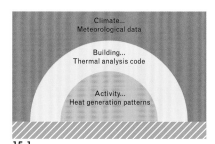

15.1

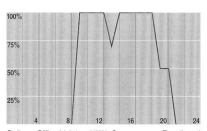

Ordinary Office Lighting 25W/m²   Time (hours)
15.2a

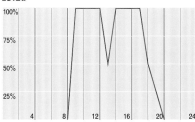

Ordinary Office Occupants 0.2 Person/m²   Time (hours)
15.2b

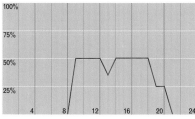

Ordinary Office Equipment 20W/m²   Time (hours)
15.2c

climate, or the local conditions, which affect the building from outside must be ascertained from surveying meteorological records. The factors that affect the building from the inside are sources of heat generation due to activities within its interior. The size and pattern over time of these heat sources must also be established. Heat flows within the thermal conduction system that is the building, under the influence of internal and external thermal excitation. It is the job of the thermal analysis code to resolve these flows (figures 15.1, 15.2a, b and c).

Meteorological Data

Buildings are required by their design to be suitable for the conditions in the region where they are located. Meteorological elements are the primary indicator of the nature of a region. As far as heat is concerned, the main meteorological factors are air temperature, humidity and sunshine, with wind, rain and cloud being of secondary importance. The National Meteorological Agency continuously measures these predominant forces and such records are available to the public. The measured data for each hour over the year can be compiled into a 'Meteorological database for thermal analysis', but this gives rise to a problem. The climate clearly varies from year to year, so if one year is chosen at will, there is no guarantee that it is representative of the region's climate. Meteorological data for a representative year must be obtained from measured data for some decades by extracting and merging together representative periods to produce a 'reference year'. The processing method developed in Japan is known as 'Akasaka's Simplified Method', and the data produced by this method is known as 'Standard meteorological data – reference year' (figure15.3).

The standard meteorological data - reference year for the total number of annual hours of 8,760 includes the following seven elements:
1. Outside air temperature
2. Outside air humidity
3. Direct solar radiation
4. Diffuse solar radiation
5. Amount of cloud
6. Wind direction
7. Wind speed

The first such set of data was prepared for Tokyo in the mid-1970s and data has been gradually built up for other regions since then. Currently, data sets have been prepared for over 800 points nationwide (figure 15.4).

Thermal Analysis Code: HASP/ACLD

The thermal response is defined as the local rate of heat flow, the room temperature and humidity at each moment in every part of the building. This can be analyzed from input data comprising the design data for the building (i.e. the cross-sectional composition and area in each part), and the seven elements described in meteorological data above plus the pattern of internal heat generation. If, at this stage, the temperature in the room is fixed (as a design condition), the process is set to find the thermal load (i.e. the amount of heat to be added to the room to maintain its specified temperature).

If the heat added to or removed from the room (by heating and cooling equipment) is set at zero for the calculation, the process is primed to find the change of temperature in the room (this is the natural room temperature).

Of these two modes of calculation, the latter is valid for predicting the interior environment that results from the introduction of natural energy such as passive solar heating. The former mode can be used to compute the hourly thermal loads for the whole year, and when divided by the floor area, amount to the Perimeter Annual Load (PAL) as defined in the Energy Conservation Law. When assessing the energy performance of the building design, the lower figure is judged as an indicator of optimum energy efficiency (figures 15.5a, b and 15.6).

The Expanded Degree Day:
A Simple Expression of Thermal Performance

Numerous case studies using HASP/ACLD have revealed the key factors that determine the energy-saving performance of a building's shell. Using this discovery, this seemingly complex problem can be resolved into relationships between four parameters. These four parameters, when linked to the full range

15.3 A sample of a
standard weather data-test
reference year – Tokyo.

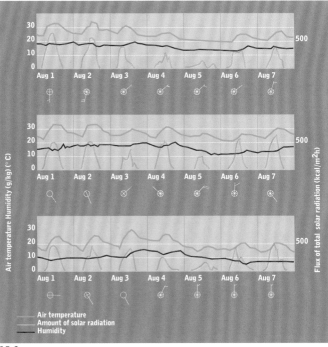

15.3

of thermal analysis described above, can be arranged as follows:

a) Meteorological data ... Extended degree day EDD

b) Thermal analysis code ... Average heat transmittance $\bar{k}$, average solar radiation penetration rate $\bar{\tau}$

c) Heat generation pattern ... Average internal heat generation density g

Thus, the four parameters are:

• The extended degree day, which represents the meteorological data for the region.

• The average heat transmittance $\bar{k}$, which represents the response to the difference in indoor and outdoor temperatures in the heat conduction response relationship.

• The average solar radiation penetration rate, which represents the response to the amount of impinging solar radiation.

• The average hourly value for internal heat generation, which represents internal heat generation.

The Perimeter Annual Load (PAL) can approximately express the relationship between these parameters as a simple linear affinity. These four parameters are extremely important tools in the application of energy-saving design. The average heat transmittance rate used here is an area-weighted average of the heat transmittance through each portion of the building shell (outer wall, glass window etc.) The average solar radiation penetration rate is calculated similarly (figure 15.7).

The PAL Chart: Applications to the Design of the Building Shell

The PAL chart is a graphical expression of the calculation process for the extended degree day method. The chart's main element is a contour graph of PAL values plotted with the average heat transmittance of the exterior parts of the building on the y axis, and the average solar radiation penetration rate on the x axis. At the bottom and left of the diagram are two graphical calculation elements for the effects of specific design measures such as shell window area percentage, exterior wall insulation thickness and window shading. To correct for differences in internal heat generation density, the reference temperature on the right axis is used.

This chart allows the architect to easily find the PAL value for a design. To give the design concerned better performance, it should be moved to a position deeper into the valley of the contour line, so the properties of the design can be varied. Alternatively, the target PAL value can be taken as the starting point, and the designer can work backwards to find a composition of the external shell that will satisfy that condition. PAL charts are prepared for each region and external orientation, so their main elements differ. Therefore these various charts allow a detailed examination of the optimum shell configuration for each region and orientation (figure 15.8).

The thermal analysis of buildings is an important process in an increasing array of high technologies developed to quantify the built environment—from the micro to the macro level. The analytical procedures described here are basic methods that can also be used in combination with dynamic simulation and air flow analysis (see Chapter 13) and even with more human response-oriented methods such as PMV (Predicted Mean Vote: see Chapter 12). Such technologies allow the architect and building engineer access to valuable data that in turn influence decisions made in the design process. Furthermore, prediction techniques provide accurate evaluations of how buildings and cities impact on the environment, and are essential tools in the practice of sustainable architecture.

15.4 Areas of Japan for
which standard
meteorological data has
been developed.

15.5a and b
Convolutional calculation
using the response factor
method.

15.6 Temperature and
heating for a modelled house:
Case A – No insulation:
temperature and load are
effected directly by outdoor
conditions

Case B – Internal insulation:
the load is reduced, although
the temperature sometimes
changes beyond the proper
range between 22–26°C

Case C – External insulation :
the temperature stays steady
due to its heat storage mass.
However, it will not recover
easily to the proper state once
the temperature is beyond
the range.

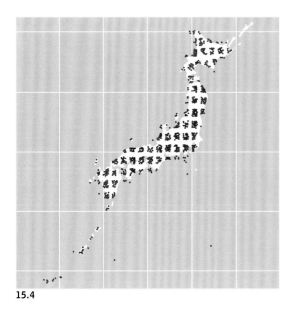

15.4

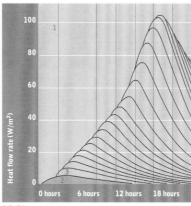

15.5a

1 Resolution of external
temperature into a series of
triangular waves.
2 Triangular wave 1.
3 Triangular wave 2.

15.5b

1 Interactive calculation
using response factor and
series of triangular waves.
2 Response due to triangular
wave 1.
3 Response due to triangular
wave 2.

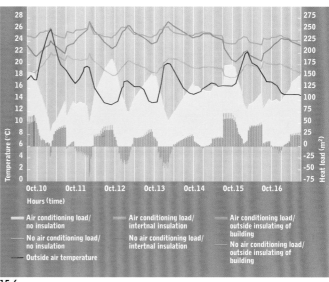

15.6

15.7 The extended degree day is the area (D and E) enclosed by reference temperature (C and J) and the average sol air temperature (F). The sol air temperature is found by adding the sun's contribution to the air temperature. The reference temperature is found by subtracting the amount of internal heat generation from the design temperature for air-conditioning.

Key
A. Design temperature 26°C for cooling.
B. Temperature increase due to internal heat generation.
C. Reference temperature 20°C for cooling
D. Extended heating degree day.
E. Extended cooling degree day.
F. Average sol air temperature.
G. Converted temperature rise from solar radiation.
H. Average air temperature.
I. Design temperature 22°C for heating.
J. Reference temperature 16°C for heating.

15.8 Example of PAL chart.

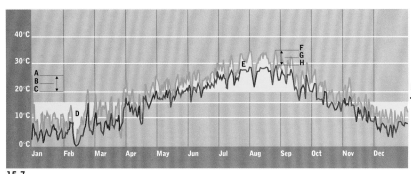

15.7

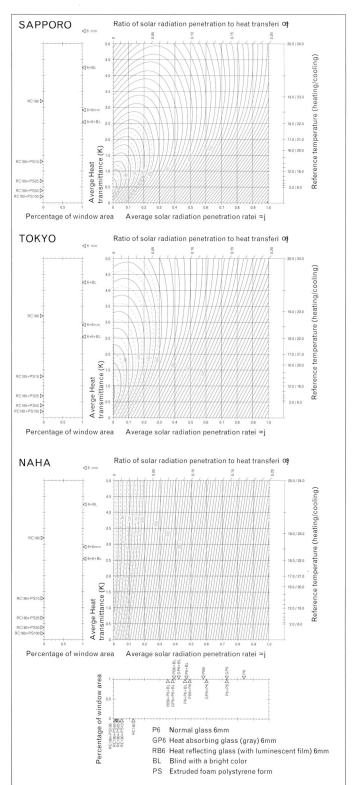

15.8

Lake Biwa Museum and
UNEP International
Environmental Technology
Center, Shiga Prefecture.
Lake water as the key
component in the
architectural scheme.

Tatsuya Inooka
General Manager,
Environmental
Engineering Group,
Nikken Sekkei, Osaka

Simulation of Air Conditioning Systems

Simulation as an Architectural Tool

The process of simulation is defined as 'a training device or a research approach that duplicates artificially the conditions likely to be encountered under certain circumstances or operations'. A general example would be a flight simulator, a highly effective tool used in pilot education, which creates an environment on the ground replicating the experience of controlling an aircraft. Such processes also train pilots and flight engineers to handle mechanical failures and a wide range of emergency situations.

As an investigative protocol for architectural design, simulation with aid of high-powered computers has rapidly become a standard twentieth century tool in building sciences. The most common application of simulation uses devised experiments that imitate the action of the actual processes under investigation. Simulations can also create fairly accurate mathematical or theoretical models of building systems to predict functional and structural outcomes in planning and design. The solutions are then subjected to numerical and other types of analyses to prove the validity of new theories or assumptions. Simulations are also used in architecture to assess whether a designer's plan is feasible and how it will impact on the environment. Not all architectural simulation models involve computers. However, since architects and engineers cannot match their calculating and memory powers in such processes, they are utilized wherever complex and voluminous calculations are required.

From Heat Load Calculation to Air Conditioning System Simulation

The unsteady state thermal load of buildings (as described earlier in Chapter 15) and the challenges it presents has spurred the development of energy-saving analysis and made a great contribution to improving the quality of design. Thermal analysis now makes it possible to evaluate and monitor thermal loads according to year-round meteorological conditions and the functional use of a building. It also enables us to accurately analyze the effect of mass heat stored in the fabric, the efficacy of insulation, the transmission/reflective properties of window glass, blinds, eaves and other shading devices. The same methods can also be used to calculate thermal loads in the design of highly original buildings where the architect employs innovative concepts and non-traditional forms.

Advances in analytical simulation are important because, even though there are differences in the specific conditions and architectural approaches, all buildings, whatever their design, obey the same rules for heat transmission. We must remember that heat loads simply enumerate the amount of heat required in a space to support a specific temperature. They are not indicative of energy consumption in terms of gas, electricity and water. For example, there is a two-part criterion under the Energy Saving Law by which the Perimeter Annual Load (PAL) has become the energy-saving standard for building heat loads, while CEC/AC rating is the equivalent for air conditioning equipment. A given heat load and the energy consumption required to remove it from the thermal environment varies, depending on the quality of the building's design, and how the air conditioning system is controlled. System simulation for air conditioning analysis is essential in predicting air conditioning energy consumption loads, a comfortable thermal environment and the overall energy/cost saving strategies of a building.

In 1985 this author was a member of a research group from the Japan Building Mechanical and Electrical Engineers Association, and developed a standardized air conditioning system simulation program called HASP/ACSS/8502. Simultaneously, Dr. Yoh Matsuo (the author of Chapter 15) also created an enhanced program for simulation. This program calculated thermal loads known as HASP/ACLD/8501. Together, these two simulation methods came to be known as HASP/ACLD/ACSS (figure 16.1).

Previous simulations also had the ability to calculate heat loads and energy consumption rates, but were limited by equipment properties. Their intent and objectives were similar to HASP/ACLD/ACSS. However, these older methods had to assume an equipment capacity in order to calculate a load (an amount of heat to be eliminated) for a particular room. This proved difficult since the equipment capacity is the potential effectiveness of an air conditioning system that can't be known without first running an air conditioning simulation. It's also impossible to analyze the system's intrinsic properties, such as zoning relationships, mixing losses, and the impact of over or under-capacity in the

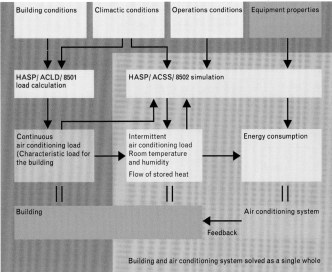

16.1

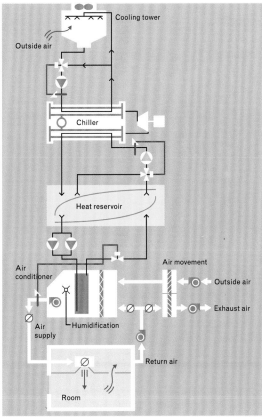

16.2

heating and cooling equipment. Such limitations were unavoidable, given the low speed performance of the computers available at the time.

HASP/ACLD/ACSS found the answer to many of these dilemmas by viewing the environmental factors of a space as an integrated whole, instead of separating the room and its physical features from the air conditioning system and solving for each aspect individually. This landmark development in the analytical process made it possible to allow for transitional overload states. The continuous air conditioning load can be described as characteristic and specific to the built space. The ACLD for 8501 was able to locate continuous air conditioning loads.

The ACSS side of the program calculates factors related to the air conditioning system, such as the operation schedule and how it's controlled. This two-part simulation working in unison can find a thermal solution for any interior and its air conditioning system by approaching the necessary and unique requirements of the space as a single totality.

The Results of a Resolved Totality

An example of this two-fold method would be as follows: in an overload state, if the chiller becomes overburdened and can't handle the load, the temperature of the chilled water rises. This reduces the air conditioner's capacity to extract the load from the room. As a result, the room temperature also rises. When this happens, the load is diminished as a result. The increased room temperature is returned to the air conditioning system with return air. Eventually, the system, as a whole, reaches an equilibrium where the temperature, humidity, heat, air and flow volume are balanced out.

An overload is a commonplace event. Every morning when an air conditioning system starts running, it encounters heat that's already accumulated in the fabric of the building, so the system is inevitably overloaded. Simulation aids in assessing this initial 'ambient' load and helps define how much collected heat has to be factored in to the system's optimum operating capacities. The ACSS method makes it possible to recreate a more accurate and realistic model of energy consumption. Consequently, one can now analyze the indoor environment, its thermal load and the energy consumed with enhanced precision.

System Simulation

An air conditioning system encompasses a large array of devices—even the room is counted among its elements. The list also includes air conditioners, thermal storage, heat pumps, chillers, boilers and cooling towers. The air conditioner comprises a cooling water coil, a humidifier, a fan and other constituents. Fans, ducts, diffusers, pumps and pipes are the transport system, which serve to link the various devices. Efficient performance of the system involves temperature and humidity settings; control of air volume and flow; outlet air temperature; the outside air intake, the on/off mode of heat source equipment, the number of units in operation, and other operational controls and scheduling functions.

The properties of individual devices are already known, but their action, once they are incorporated into a system, needs to be discovered. Optimum performance depends on how well the system matches the loads, how the devices are assembled, how they are controlled and other factors. Simulations developed to manage such a range of variables are commonly called 'system simulations' (figure 16.2).

The Basic Form of the Subsystem

There are many types of simulation models for air conditioning systems. For example, the model for a typical room uses an RF (response factor) and a WF (weighting factor) in line with an unsteady state heat load theory in order to calculate the temperature and humidity in the room, together with the stored heat flow. The model for water cooling coils and the cooling tower in the transmission of moist heat can solve temporal changes in the temperature distribution for the heat reservoir. Models for the heat source equipment, the fan and the pump approximate their properties as a polynomial. Thus a variety of model types do exist side by side, each utilized in the investigation and collection of valuable data.

Figure 16.3 illustrates the basic form of a subsystem. It has given conditions from downstream (flow volume GL, intake temperature TLi), given

16.3 Subsystem.
16.4 The entire system.
16.5 A simulation example of
energy consumption in an air
conditioning system. Addition
of total heat exchangers is
effective in winter. Cooling by
outside air is sufficient in
intermediate seasons.

Variable air volume in the
system fans halves energy
consumption. In April cooling
with outside air at constant
air volume is more effective
than using VAV to restrict
air volume.

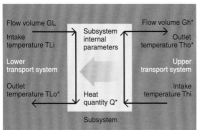

16.3

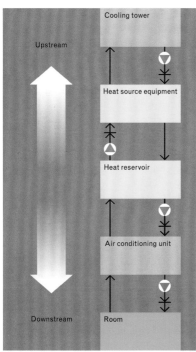

16.4

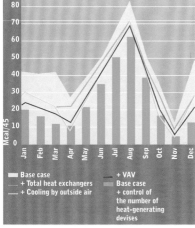

16.5

conditions from upstream (intake temperature Thi) and internal parameters (capacity Q), set temperature of the outlet temperature (TLo etc.) all acting to satisfy the demand load Q*.

If the capacity Q meets the demand load Q*, the flow rate Gh* on the upstream side is varied within the control range, and the outlet temperature TLo on the downstream side is able to achieve the set temperature. However, if capacity Q cannot meet demand load Q, the outlet temperature on the downstream side TLo* will fluctuate.

This is the basic form for an active model type that controls heat source equipment and cooling coils. In contrast, a room's thermal storage tanks and other such elements have no control action of their own and are defined as passive models. As such, their outlet conditions are variable. A cooling tower is basically passive, but it has a minimum outlet temperature that is controlled, so it can be called an intermediate type

Simulation Model for a Cooling Coil

The cooling water coil could be considered an example of a subsystem model. The coil uses chilled water supplied from the heat source equipment to create a cool airflow in the room. This is also the basic form for a model of heat conduction. However, cooling is accompanied by dehumidification, so the coils are classified as either dry or wet parts. The given conditions from the downstream side (the room) are the airflow volume Ga, intake air temperature and humidity Ta1 and Xa1. The given conditions from upstream (the heat source) is the intake water temperature Tc1. The internal parameters include the coil surface area So, the heat transfer coefficients Uw and Ud (coefficients for wind and flow speed), and the control range for flow rate Gc. The outlet air factors Ta3 and Ha3 are required to deal with the heat load downstream.

Under these conditions, simultaneous equations are solved so that the coil area is S = So.

Where there is a light load that the coil can handle, the flow rate Gx is adjusted within the control range. When an overload occurs that the coil can't handle, the outlet air condition Ha3* is not satisfied, even when the flow volume G* reaches maximum.

The Entire System

The system as a whole begins with the given conditions from upstream as its initial values, while the calculation starts from the downstream subsystem. Information is passed through the transport system as the calculation proceeds successively upstream. If the given circumstances change due to an overload, the calculation is performed repeatedly until it converges at a solution (figure 16.4).

An Example of a System Simulation Calculation

The calculation illustrated in Figure 16.5 is for an office space with a floor area of 10,000m². The basic case is one where no consideration at all has been given to energy saving strategies. The graph plots the reduction in primary energy consumption for each month as a result of adding: 1) heat exchangers, 2) cooling by outside air, 3) variable air volume, 4) control of the number of heat-generating devices.

Energy saving measures do not necessarily yield uniform results. A given measure can be effective in one case and not in another. Many of the available measures include elements that conflict with each other. Ideally, a good design should minimize the disadvantage and maximize the advantages, but that is difficult to achieve in practice.

The addition of total heat exchangers is very proficient in winter but can also be effective throughout the year. Cooling by outside air is a useful alternative during intermediate seasons. Variable air volume reduces the energy consumption by half in the system's fans but the overall effect appears slight. This occurs because the system uses VAV together with fan coils at the perimeter. In spring it's more efficient to utilize cooling with outside air at a constant air volume than to use VAV to restrict air volume (figure 16.5).

Dynamic Simulation

HASP/ACLD/ACSS is a simulation mainly used to calculate energy consumption. Dynamic simulation differs by focusing on the detailed recreation of control actions. HVACSIM is known as the leading dynamic simulation

16.6 Example of a system configuration for dynamic simulation.
Outside air drawn in through the system passes through fan F and cooled by the cooling coil (C/C). At this stage, the opening of the cold water valve is varied by controller C3. This adjusts the flow of cold water from the water chiller. The chilled air is fed to the interior to adjust the room temperature. These temperature changes can be plotted in graphs, based on simulation results.
16.7a The calculated result from the dynamic simulation of room temperature.
16.7b The temperature of the room varies as the aperture of the cold water valve is adjusted by the controller.

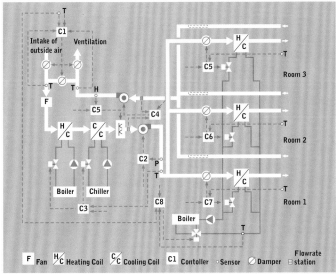

16.6

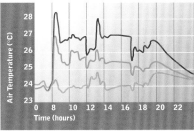

16.7a

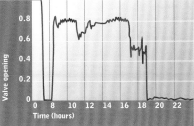

16.7b

program. Its Japanese version is HVACSIM+ VER. 8.1 (J) (figures 16.6. and 16.7).

The following lists the differences between HASP/ ACLD/ ACSS and dynamic simulations.

With HASP/ACLD/ACSS, the control model is on a macro scale and locates the balance action at intervals of one hour. It repeats this for the 8,760 hours of one year to detect the amount of energy consumption. Dynamic simulation analyses each control action and takes time constants into account within its model.

	HASP/ACLD/ACSS	Dynamic Simulation
Objective	Energy analysis	Action analysis (commissioning)
Calculation time interval	Hourly intervals over the 8,760 hours of the year	Short-term calculation over minute and second intervals
Action	Hourly average heat and flow volume balance	The effects of the actions themselves
Heat capacity	Static model, other than for rooms, pipes and heat storage	Heat capacities for all elements can be considered
Input data	List of devices	Detailed information

The time interval for calculation is the minute or the second. For example, if the flow rate in the cooling water coil is constricted, ACSS analysis determines the state of heat, flow rate and temperature for the entire system's equilibrium. Dynamic simulation recreates in detail the variations in the opening of the valve that constricts the flow rate and the sum of the flow rate itself.

Every simulation must be modelled and applied according to its objective. Dynamic simulation is currently used more in research than in design work. It requires enormous amounts of calculation processing, as well as detailed input data. However, dynamic simulation is a powerful tool that can be used for commissioning, such as checking systems for BOFD (Building Optimization and Fault Detection) and also for faults before the project reaches the construction stage. This is a field where we can expect to see great progress in the future.

Koichi Kaiho
Senior Engineer,
Nikken Sekkei,
Tokyo

Quantitative Evaluation Techniques in the Analysis of Natural Light

Light as a Building Material – The Solar Focus of Architecture

For centuries architects have enjoyed a special affinity for natural light and, no matter where the built space exists, they have always understood its unique behaviour within their own geographic region. The innumerable man-made sites dedicated to the sun all over the world reaffirm architecture's relationship with luminance. Designing with and for available light also extends its reach in the interaction with other building materials and their expression. An example of this would be the shaded tiled cloisters of Moorish gardens with fountains and ponds carefully placed to reflect sunlight.

However, over the past fifty years, the use of natural light as a building component has been sadly diminished by other architectural objectives. Many modern buildings are surfaced with steel and densely tinted glass that limit the entry of daylight. Occupants of such structures often spend their entire working hours under fluorescent strips. The result of such design is a drain on energy resources and impacts on the physiological condition of building users.

Considering and implementing natural light into architectural design has a tremendous influence on the eventual conformation of a building. It generates an array of functional strategies such as room height, window size, the types of glass used, orientation to compass points, human traffic paths, light shelves, skylights, eaves, verandahs and landscaping.

As well as simply keeping a room illuminated during the day, natural light is also vitally important for creating a fulfilling environment. Human beings are highly phototropic creatures, right to the core of their brains and the light-activated firing of neurons behind the eyes. Not just any form of light satisfies these physiological requirements—natural light is considered to be the most beneficial. Given the encompassing and innate need of people to function in the presence of natural light, it's important to re-assess the integration of this abundant resource in building design as a way of creating a more benign living and working environment (figure 17.1).

The use of natural light in working and dwelling spaces has three main effects. People have an historical phenomenal relationship with sunlight so persistent and essential that the body has evolved its own symbiotic and individuated responses to this stimulus. When communities lived with little or no artificial lighting, the sun was also an essential source of indoor lighting. Even today, deploying sunlight throughout buildings can substantially reduce the energy consumption and costs of artificial light (figure 17.2). Natural light varies constantly with changes of season, time and weather. It brings the outdoor environment into the building interior, endowing a space with expansion and openness. Natural light is harmonious. Fluorescent light supplies most contemporary buildings with artificial illumination but it has none of the qualities of natural light.

The wavelengths of light visible to the human eye are between 360 and 720 nanometers. Natural visible light is distributed uniformly in a range between blue (short-wavelength light) and red (long-wavelength light), so all the colours are rendered accurately. Fluorescent light has spikes of intensity only at certain wavelengths. As a result, some colours can appear unnatural and distorted.

This is not just a problem with colour perception. It also impacts on human physiology in phenomena such as rhythms of sleeping and waking. In the course of evolution, the human eye has adapted physiologically to natural light and prolonged isolation away from its stimulus is thought to cause a variety of health problems. When one considers all the attributes of natural light, it is clearly very important to make the most appropriate use of this essential element in the design of buildings.

Methods for Quantifying and Analyzing Natural Light

In order to make effective use of natural light in architectural planning we must have an adequate grasp of its properties. Design that correctly incorporates daylight into the interior space, without glare or intense fluctuation, requires the quantitative analysis of natural light. Such analyses can broadly be divided into the predictive and the measured evaluation of the light environment.

Predicting the Brightness of Spaces
Computer Analysis of Three-dimensional Luminance Distribution

Prediction means the simulation of the luminance distribution in a building at the design stage, based on the planned forms of the interior. This simulation

17.1 Natural light plays an
important role in a fulfilling
environment.

17.2 Use of abundant natural
light allows major reductions
in the use of artificial light
sources: natural lighting from
both sides.

17.1

17.2

allows the optimization of design elements such as the building plan, open and closed spaces, window locations and all light entry points, the cross section, the specifications of surface finishes and other factors.

The most widely used yardstick of brightness is the flux density on a horizontal plane. However, the perceived brightness in a space must be evaluated from the luminance distribution within the subject's field of view. The human eye perceives the brightness of a space in terms of luminance rather than flux density. Therefore evaluation of the perceived brightness of a space, due to natural light or light from any other source, demands knowledge of the three-dimensional luminance distribution. (However, flux density is an important measure for visibility of the viewed subject of visual work on a desktop.)

Figure 17.2 shows the general brightness distribution on a horizontal plan for a space lit by natural light and the luminance distribution analyzed in three dimensions for the same area. It is not possible to ascertain from the brightness on the horizontal plane how much light from the window reaches the walls and the ceiling. This means there is no correct way of evaluating the light environment as seen by the human eye. However, the three-dimensional analysis can easily discern the level of brightness over the whole field of view. Figure 17.3 illustrates the energy distribution of natural and fluoresent light (3-wavelenght type).

Figure 17.4 depicts three-dimensional analysis, made at the design stage, of natural light and its effect in the working area of an office building. When light enters from only one side, there is a substantial difference in luminance between the window location and the opposite side of the space. When light enters from both sides of the building, the natural lighting result is highly effective, and the space is evenly lit, with little difference in luminance. The use of natural light was a vital feature of this building's design, and, as a result of the analysis, the decision was made to allow light to enter from both sides of the office.

Measuring the Brightness of Spaces
Measurement of the Luminance Distribution in a Space using a Digital Camera

Measurement of the light environment in existing buildings and in newly completed projects provides essential feedback to the architect and helps further the design process. This evaluation requires simple but highly precise measurement techniques. For a normal calculation of brightness, the flux density distribution can be measured by a light meter, while a luminance meter is used to determine the luminance of the interior. These methods have their limitations and require a great deal of time and effort to gauge the entire field of view. It is also very difficult to get an accurate reading of luminance distribution in a three-dimensional space. However, newly developed digital cameras make it possible to capture and convert images into luminance distribution for a room or a building, similar to the way it is perceived by the human eye. This method is simple and very accurate. Finding the luminance distribution within the field of view requires converting the digitized data from CCD pixels by using a conversion table.

Figure 17.5a is a luminance distribution for a naturally lit space measured by this method. Figure 17.5b shows the same space, predicted at the design stage by simulation. Figure 17.6 illustrates the natural light as calculated using a digital camera and a simple model of the space built at the design stage. The use of digital cameras in these various methods of analyses has made it possible to find the complex distribution of luminance within a space quickly and easily. It also allows comparisons between predictions by simulation and measured evaluation after the building is completed.

Predicting the Performance of Natural Light in a Building
Analysis of Light Intake Throughout the Year

The methods described so far for the evaluation of luminance examine a space from one segment in time, but in a real building the light environment changes from moment to moment. The design of a building requires comparing various building forms with their efficacy as measured by their strategies in utilizing natural light. For example, eaves above windows block direct solar radiation, but if the eaves are too deep the light reaching the interior will be reduced. On the other hand, deep eaves mounted on window frames reduce the amount of time shades are drawn against direct sun, thus lengthening the hours in which natural light is available. This balance varies, depending on the climate conditions at the building site, the form and orientation of the building, and other factors.

17.3 Energy distribution of
natural and fluorescent light
(3-wavelength type).
17.4 Examples of the
3-dimensional analysis of
the effects of natural light.

17.4a One-sided natural
lighting.
17.4b Two-sided natural
lighting.

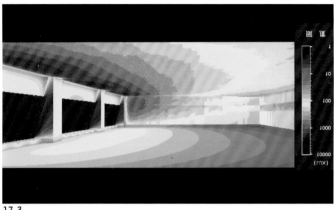

17.3

17.4a

17.4b

The latitude and location of a building changes the entry rate of light. Therefore, it influences the effect caused by the shape of eaves. For example, in Okinawa where the latitude is low, the eaves are highly effective, while in Sapporo, situated at much higher latitude, the same eaves would have a much smaller effect. Figure 17.7 illustrates the way the effect of the eaves changes with a building's orientation. It shows quantitatively how the effect of eaves varies greatly with the direction of the light entry points. This year-round statistical analysis of the light environment makes it possible to design buildings that make optimum use of natural light.

Examples of Analytical Evaluation
Case 1: Analysis of Natural Light in a Traditional Japanese Building (Prediction and Measurement)

Figures 17.8, 17.9a and 17.9b are an example of a prediction by simulation of the light environment in a room in a traditional Japanese-style building. The deep eaves keep the direct entry of sunlight down to an appropriate level and the space has an air of calm relaxation. Light reflected from the floor on the engawa (verandah) side passes through the high openwork screen to light the ceiling and soften the contrast in brightness. After the simulation was complete, a digital camera was used in a luminance measurement system to produce the data shown in figure 17.9c. The measured results largely match the luminance distribution predicted by the prior analysis, confirming the validity of the computer simulation of the light environment that was conducted at the design stage.

Case 2: Analysis of Changes in the Light Environment in Spaces along a Path

When considering the light environment inside a building, one must pay close attention to differences in the brightness between spaces. For example, everyone has experienced the temporary loss of vision that occurs on entering a dark interior directly from a bright sunlit exterior. The vision loss is caused by the sudden and extreme difference between outdoor brightness of thousands or even tens of thousands of cd/m^2 and the indoor brightness of, at best, a few hundred cd/m^2. This is not something that can be solved by lighting design alone. The skilful integration of natural light into the design at the building planning stage can reduce the contrast in brightness that a subject experiences while moving between spaces.

Figure 17.11 shows the measured changes in luminance distribution in a subject's field of view while walking in from the outside through the entrance of an office building and on to the work area. The red line on the diagram is for an ordinary building and the blue line is for one that uses natural light in the entrance and passageways. In the approach through the ordinary building, the peak variation in brightness along the route walked from outside to the working area was 70:1. Where natural light was taken into the spaces along the route walked, the peak variation was only 10:1. This is clearly a major improvement in the brightness ratio. Allowing natural light to penetrate the passageways within a building has the important benefit of automatically alleviating the problem of brightness disparity between the interior and the exterior.

Conclusion

As we have seen, the qualitative analysis and evaluation of the use of natural light in the early stages of planning and design is an extremely effective way of creating a better light environment in the completed building. In particular, with the practical development of control technologies such as automatic blinds and automatic light dimming, as well as transparent insulating materials, the peripheral technologies that enable the use of natural light in architecture have made great advances. With increasing universal concern for the degradation of the environment, there is an urgent need for design methods that will incorporate these new technologies and apply them to buildings. The quantitative evaluation of natural light is an essential tool to this end.

It's now possible to predict and measure the quantity of natural light in any proposed built space with a high degree of precision. To further this process, the visual environment, in terms of comfort, must be studied and investigated, and the results used as a guide as to what kind of light environment can be produced from the use of natural light. However, while there have been some suggested methods of assessment using glare, there has been little research on the quantitative measurement of comfort and the situation remains a difficult challenge. The two greatest research tasks in this field to date are the development of more precise methods for quantifying and evaluating natural light, and determining its impact on the visual environment.

17.5a Measurement of a naturally-lit space using a digital camera.
17.5b Computer prediction of the same naturally-lit space.

17.6 Measurement of a model of the same naturally-lit space using a digital camera. The model represents a room lit from both sides with an inclined ceiling and with the factor of overcast weather outside (illuminance equivalence = 15,000 lux on an horizontal plane). These internally visible models at 1/100 scale were built to confirm the light environment produced by natural light.
17.7 Differences in the effects of eaves with regard to the building's orientation.

17.5a

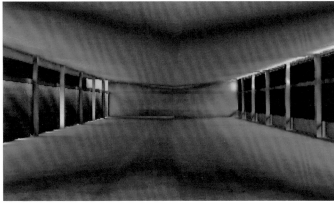
17.5b

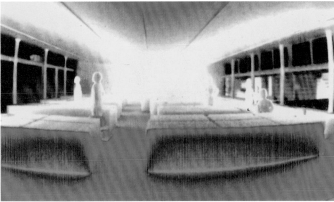
17.6

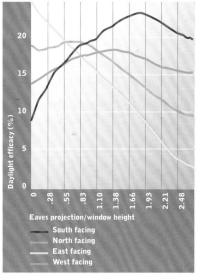
17.7

17.8 Differences in the
effects of eaves with regard to
the building's orientation –
a view of Genshinan.
17.9a Computer-generated
image of a traditional
Japanese room in Genshinan.

17.9b Computer-generated
3-dimensional prediction of
light in the room.
17.9c Measurement of a
naturally-lit space using a
digital camera.

17.8

17.9a

17.9b

17.9c

17.10 Exterior of building
using natural light.
17.11 Variations in luminance
in building passageway using
natural light.

17.10

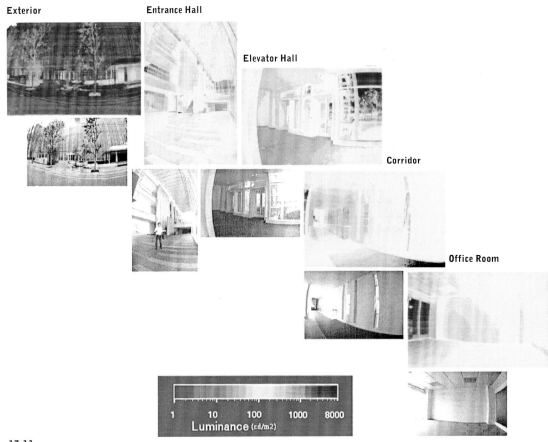

Exterior
Entrance Hall
Elevator Hall
Corridor
Office Room

Luminance (cd/m2)
1 10 100 1000 8000

17.11

Toshiharu Ikaga
Associate Professor,
The Institute of
Industrial Science,
University of Tokyo

Measurement
of Lifecycle
CO_2
in Buildings

The Impact of Buildings on the Global Environment

We design and construct buildings and endow them with an array of complex functions. We administrate them, repeatedly repair and improve them, and finally demolish them, using energy and resources at every stage throughout their life span. As a result, many wastes in solid, liquid and gaseous form are dispersed into the global environment. The rise of perilous degradations such as global warming, ozone depletion, acid rain, the dispersion of hazardous wastes and the pollution of the oceans is a harsh but well-deserved lesson in revealing to us the fragility of the world's environment. The fabric of nature simply cannot accommodate such a relentless load.

The Lifecycle Environmental Burden as Generated by a Single Building

Evaluation of the environmental burden imposed by a building requires an overall judgement based on the analysis of various load factors. Figure 18.1 illustrates a conceptual definition of the lifecycle environmental burden as the weighted average of these load factors , according to their impact on sustainable human prosperity and well-being. Ozone depletion, which is linked to skin cancer, hazardous wastes, that can rapidly bring on genetic damage in humans and their descendants, and other such environmental burdens are load factors with a substantial weight. Other problems such as global warming, that increase over time and threaten many life forms worldwide, will become the legacy of future generations, and are not necessarily any lighter. The weighting factors cannot be explained entirely by science. They are also determined by architectural intent, societal values and political judgements.

The Definition of Lifecycle CO_2

Lifecycle CO_2 is a common standard in evaluating the environmental impact of load factors in the form of global warming. Apart from CO_2, there are a number of 'greenhouse' gases such as methane and the HCFCs (Hydro-chlorofluoro-carbons) contributing to the same effect. One definition of lifecycle CO_2 only considers actual CO_2 ($LCCO_2$). However, there is the broader category ($LCCO_2*$), which includes other chemical agents (greenhouse gases) that also adversely influence and degrade the world's climate. These substances are converted to CO_2 equivalents, and categorized according to the severity of their damage capacity. In order to compare the various greenhouse gases with CO_2 in connection with global warming, the GWP (global warming potential) of each gas relative to CO_2 (which is taken as 1) is multiplied by 12/44, the ratio by weight of carbon in CO_2. The result is the conversion coefficient ß for each gas. The GWP values for the greenhouse gases associated with buildings are listed in figure 18.2. When ß is multiplied by the emission volume for each gas and the results added together, the total is the broadly defined as $LCCO_2*$.

Note: The GWP values are 100-year cumulative values, as announced by the intergovernmental committee known as the International Panel on Climate Change.

Energy Saving and Lifecycle CO_2

In the construction industry, lifecycle cost (LCC) analysis was adopted at a comparatively early stage as a method of economic evaluation. It has yielded great results as an investment guideline for property owners aiming for qualitative improvement in buildings. This analytical process made it clear that the energy cost for air conditioning, lighting and other energy applications accounted for a major share within the lifecycle cost of a building.

Among the methods available for analyzing energy consumption at the operation stage, PAL (Perimeter Annual Load) and CEC (Coefficient of Energy Consumption) have been widely used as indicators for pre-construction evaluation of the energy-saving performance of buildings. However, PAL and CEC are not methods for determining actual cost. Lifecycle CO_2 is calculated on the basis of existing methods for cost and energy performance analysis, converting costs and quantities into CO_2 emission intensities.

Lifecycle CO_2 Calculation Method

CO_2 emissions associated with a building are generated at every stage from its design through construction, operation and repair to its demolition and disposal. The lifecycle CO_2 covers the entire emission volume. As noted above the calculation of lifecycle CO_2 ($LCCO_2$) is based on LCC. For example, the unit

Life Cycle Environmental Load

$= \alpha$	CO_2 x	Green House Effect Gases
$+ \alpha$	CFCs x	Ozone Depletion Gases
$+ \alpha$	NO_2 x	Acid Rain Gases
$+ \alpha$	Toxic x	Toxic Waste Heat
$+ \alpha$	E x	Waste Heat
:		Where α = factor based on impact on sustainable future

Life Cycle CO_2 (Green House Effect Gases) kg-C **(Life Cycle CO_2 in broad sense $LCCO_2$)** ◄

$= 1$	CO_2 x	**(Life Cycle CO_2 in narrow sense $LCCO_2$)**
$+ \beta$	CFCs x	CFCs
$+ \beta$	NO_2 x	NO_2
$+ \beta$	CH_4 x	CH_4
:		Where β = global warming potential x 12/44 (carbon weight in CO_2)

Unit of Life Cycle CO_2

kg-C/year•m²	for each building design analysis
kg-C/year•person	for each building stock analysis in a country or region

18.1

Material Name	Chemical formula	Global Warming Potential (GWP)	Building-related applications
CFC 11	$CFCl_3$	4000	Refrigerant for centrifugal chillers, expanded insulating materials
Halon 1301	CF_3Br	5600	Halon fire-extingushing gas
HCFC 22	CF_2HCl	1700	Chillers, package air-conditioners, expanded insulating materials
HCFC 123	$C_2F_3HCl_2$	93	Refrigerant for centrifugal chillers
HCFC 142b	$C_2F_2H_3Cl$	2000	Expanded polystyrene
HFC 134a	CH_2FCF_3	1300	Chillers, package air-conditioners, foamed insulating materials
Sulfur fluoride	SF_6	23900	Gas-insulated circuit-breakers, gas-insulated transformers

18.2

Conditons for the Study of Energy-Saving Design Alternatives		Standard Design	Common Measures Option	Daylight Usage Option
Name of substitution options				
Buliding specification	External wall insulation (mm)	25	40	
	Effect of eaves	x	Horizontal eaves	
Equipment specification	Control of air supply volume	x	○	
	Control of minimum outside air	x	○	
	Control of outside air cooling	x	○	
	Control of lighting system by daylight		x	○
Capacity of major air conditioning equipment	Heat source (MJ/h)		3140	
	Primary pumps (kW)		11.1	
	Secondary pumps (kW)		15	
	Air conditioning equipment — Air flow (m3/hm2)			
	Air supply fan (k/W)			
	Air return fan (k/W)			

18.3

cost of the building materials is replaced with a CO_2 emission volume per unit weight of building material. For energy consumption, the CO_2 generation volume per unit of heat is used in place of the unit fuel cost. For consumption of services, the CO_2 emission volume per unit price, calculated approximately, is used as the base unit. Thus, the lifecycle CO_2 emission volume is derived from these conversions.

LCC = Unit x material quantity

+ Energy unit cost x amount of energy used

+ Service price + LCCO₂ = CO_2 generation volume per unit weight

x material weight + CO_2 generation volume per unit heat x amount of heat

+ CO_2 generation volume per unit cost x service price + ...

CO₂ Emission Intensity

A building's lifetime consumption of goods and services covers many factors besides materials and fuel. A CO_2 emission intensity must be defined for each in order to find LCCO₂. However, the substance elements of building construction are products that combine a wide variety of materials produced by other industries, and it would be impractical to analyze each of these component materials. Therefore a range of CO_2 emission intensities, such as that per unit weight of each building material, has been estimated from the input-output table of industrial relationships. This is a collection of statistical data listing the values of transactions between each of Japan's industries. Figure 18.4 lists the CO_2 emission intensities estimated in this way for a number of important building materials.

Case Study of Lifecycle CO₂ in an Office Building

The following represents a sample calculation for an office building(figure 18.5 and 18.6).

Outline of the Office Building under Study

1. Location: Tokyo (using the annual time-based meteorological data published by the Society of Heating, Air-conditioning and Sanitary Engineers of Japan)
2. Total floor area: 7741 m²
3. Area of standard floor: 968 m² (of which the effective floor area is 737 m²)
4. Number of floors and floor height: +7-1, floor height 3800 mm, ceiling height 2600 mm
5. Structure: Steel frame and steel reinforced concrete
6. Exterior finish: Ceramic tile
7. Electrical equipment: High-voltage transformer equipment situated in the basement
8. Air conditioning equipment: Heat pump air chiller (HCFC22 refrigerant) Two air conditioning units on each floor, single-duct CAV or VAV method.
   Ventilation for toilets, boiler room, basement mechanical room, EV mechanical room
9. Sanitation equipment: Water reception tank in the basement and high-level water tank on the roof. Interior dry risers
10. Elevator Equipment: Three elevators

The Breakdown of Lifecycle CO₂

Figure 18.7 shows the breakdown of LCCO₂ for a standard office building. CO_2 related to the energy consumed in the air conditioning system, lighting and other services accounts for more than 50% of the total. This demonstrates the importance of implementing measures to reduce operational energy consumption (energy-saving design and responsible management) for the reduction of CO_2. The emission volume associated with the initial design was less than 1%. Even if twice as much effort and expense were expended on the design stage, with a corresponding doubling of the CO_2 emission at that point, the overall effect would be beneficial, assuming the additional design work secured a substantial reduction in the building's LCCO₂.

It has been proved that energy use in the operational process of a building accounts for a large share of the overall consumption. However, the volume of leakage from foamed insulation materials (HCFC142b), air conditioning and heating refrigerant (HCFC22), when converted by the corresponding global warming potentials to their CO_2 equivalent for LCCO₂* (the broader definition

18.4 CO₂ emission
intensity levels of materials
during their production
and distribution.

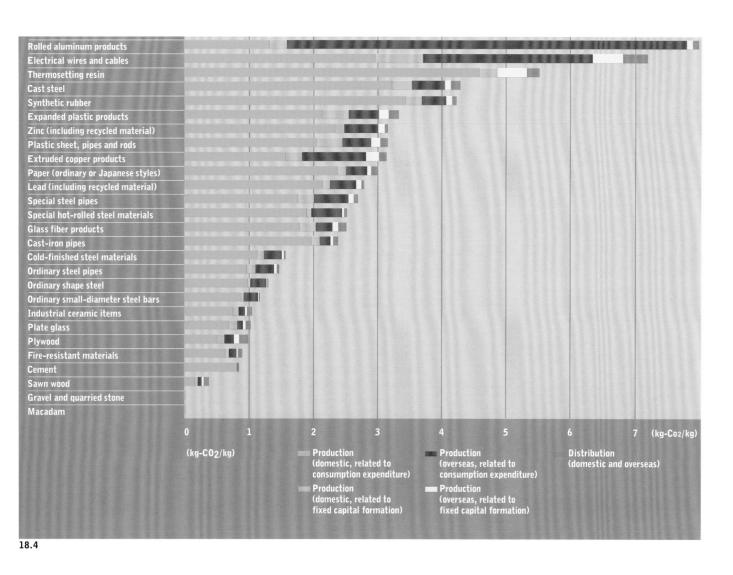

Rolled aluminum products	
Electrical wires and cables	
Thermosetting resin	
Cast steel	
Synthetic rubber	
Expanded plastic products	
Zinc (including recycled material)	
Plastic sheet, pipes and rods	
Extruded copper products	
Paper (ordinary or Japanese styles)	
Lead (including recycled material)	
Special steel pipes	
Special hot-rolled steel materials	
Glass fiber products	
Cast-iron pipes	
Cold-finished steel materials	
Ordinary steel pipes	
Ordinary shape steel	
Ordinary small-diameter steel bars	
Industrial ceramic items	
Plate glass	
Plywood	
Fire-resistant materials	
Cement	
Sawn wood	
Gravel and quarried stone	
Macadam	

0   1   2   3   4   5   6   7   (kg-Co2/kg)

(kg-CO₂/kg)

Production
(domestic, related to
consumption expenditure)

Production
(overseas, related to
consumption expenditure)

Distribution
(domestic and overseas)

Production
(domestic, related to
fixed capital formation)

Production
(overseas, related to
fixed capital formation)

18.4

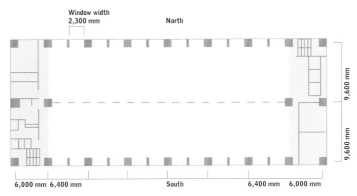

18.5

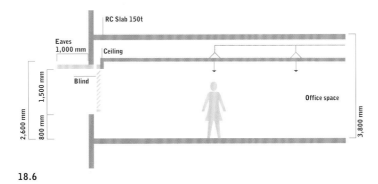

18.6

of lifecycle CO_2), their share equals nearly 10% of the $LCCO_2$ value for CO_2 alone. This rivals CO_2 emission volume for air conditioning used in heating operations. Expanded insulation materials leak 12% of their total emission during the expansion process, and the other 88% during their disposal. Therefore, even if thicker insulation materials achieve a reduction in air conditioning-related CO_2, any failure to recover HCFC142b during disposal could easily cancel out the effect of the energy saving.

A 15% Reduction through Energy Saving Measures

The largest element within the lifecycle CO_2 of a building is usually the CO_2 emission associated with operational energy consumption. Figure 18.8 shows the results of a year-round energy consumption simulation conducted for the conditions shown earlier in the sample calculation for an office building. The upper bar graph is for the standard floor with the air conditioning power consumption, for both air heating and movement, accounting for approximately a 50% share. The next largest share is the approximately 25% used by power consumption for lighting. This emphasizes the importance of energy-saving measures targeting air conditioning and lighting.

As the building study shows, the common measures option for energy saving in air conditioning achieves a 22% reduction in energy consumption. Daylight usage measures bring the combined electricity consumption saving to 29%, compared to the standard design, without sacrificing comfort. Figure 18.9 presents the results when $LCCO_2$ is re-calculated to reflect these changes. The top bar graph uses figures for the standard design. The second bar graph is for a building where energy saving measures, including increased insulation and natural ventilation have been thoroughly implemented throughout the plant and in its equipment. These measures entail some increase in the CO_2 associated with construction, repairs, improvements and demolition, but they still achieve a significant reduction of 15% in $LCCO_2$.

A 25% Reduction through Increased Building Longevity

The third bar graph in figure 18-9 depicts the results of measures taken to lengthen the life span of the building. By allowing ample margins in structural aspects such as the floor area, the height between floors and floor loading, the building can be made flexible enough to meet the demands of changing functions in the future. The assumption is that, after construction, the building will be repeatedly remodelled in its equipment, services and interior finishes to meet the demands of the times, remaining in use for at least 100 years. This reduces the frequency of replacement construction, raising the overall reduction in $LCCO_2$ to 25%.

A 28% Reduction through the Use of Ecological Materials

The fourth graph in figure 18.9 shows the situation where environment-friendly materials are used as widely as possible. This strategy includes the use of: recycled materials for structural steel elements, steel finishing panels, aluminium sash windows, tiles containing recycled glass, bricks made from dredged soil, and the utilization of natural materials such as stone and wood in the interiors and around the building's landscape. Equipment and interior finishes are replaced more frequently than structural elements, so it is particularly important to promote the use of recycled materials for such applications. As a realistic option in this situation, only the use of blast furnace cement, a by-product of steel manufacturing, was taken into account in the calculation. In figure 18.10 it is evident that the CO_2 emission intensity of blast furnace cement is about 50% lower than that of Portland cement. The calculation shows a 28% reduction in $LCCO_2$, once the use of blast furnace cement is included as shown in figure 18.9.

A 32% Reduction through Appropriate Waste Disposal

Waste disposal is another aspect where judicious measures are essential in reducing the environmental burden. Figure 18.9 illustrates that gases with very high global warming potential are consistently used in building materials. Even a small quantity of these gases can have a large impact on global warming. Either CFCs should not be used in foamed insulating materials and air conditioning refrigerants, or they should be carefully recovered on disposal. If either of these steps are implemented effectively they can bring the overall reduction in $LCCO_2$ down to 32%.

18.7 LCCO₂ breakdown for
a standard office building
design.
18.8 Calculated year-round
electrical power consumption.
18.9 The effect of measures
taken in reducing cumulative
LCCO₂.

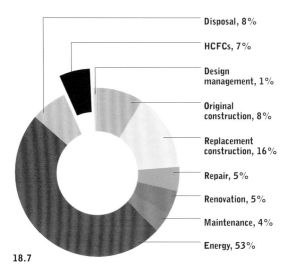

Disposal, 8%

HCFCs, 7%

Design
management, 1%

Original
construction, 8%

Replacement
construction, 16%

Repair, 5%

Renovation, 5%

Maintenance, 4%

Energy, 53%

18.7

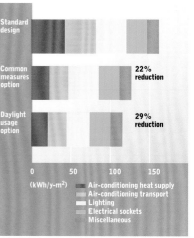

Standard
design

Common
measures
option

22%
reduction

Daylight
usage
option

29%
reduction

| | 0 | 50 | 100 | 150 |

(kWh/y-m²) ▪ Air-conditioning heat supply
▪ Air-conditioning transport
▪ Lighting
▪ Electrical sockets
▪ Miscellaneous

18.8

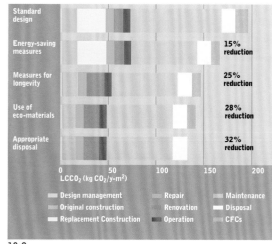

Standard
design

Energy-saving
measures

15%
reduction

Measures for
longevity

25%
reduction

Use of
eco-materials

28%
reduction

Appropriate
disposal

32%
reduction

| 0 | 50 | 100 | 150 | 200 |

LCCO₂ (kg CO₂/y-m²)

▪ Design management   ▪ Repair   ▪ Maintenance
▪ Original construction ▪ Renovation   ▪ Disposal
▪ Replacement Construction ▪ Operation   ▪ CFCs

18.9

18.10 Comparison of CO₂
emission intensities between
Portland cement and blast
furnace cement.

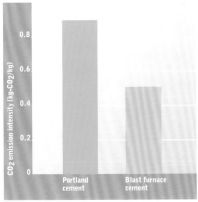

18.10

The Evaluation of Environmental Impact

The methods described here for reducing $LCCO_2$ prevalence limits their consideration to buildings and how the design and function impacts on global warming. Climate degradation was chosen as the starting point for analyzing buildings as conduits of CO_2 and $LCCO_2$ emission, mainly because it is a major and increasing environmental menace. Its extent and severity have been agreed upon internationally under the Framework Convention on Climate Change, and it was possible to assemble the relevant data quickly. Databases of boundary conditions for energy consumption volume, SO_x, and NO_x, have at last been brought up to the standard of those for CO_2. It is now possible to conduct impact assessment calculations for fossil fuel depletion, acidification and other effects of these substances. In the future, databases will be expanded to cover water pollution, industrial wastes and other environmental detritus, which will allow their constituents to be converted into emission intensities for use in the same calculation approach as that described for $LCCO_2$. The outcome of such analyses will broaden the range of points considered in the Lifecycle Assessment (LCA) of a building, making it possible to conduct a more comprehensive environmental impact assessment.

Authors'
Biographies

Part I Introduction and Essay

Eiji Maki, Dr Eng., JIA
Born in 1935 and educated at the Graduate School of the University of Tokyo,
Dr Maki is an architect and engineer of building services. He has served as the
President of Nikken Sekkei since 1993. He holds a degree of Doctor of
Engineering from the University of Tokyo and is a Registered Consultant
Engineer. Since joining Nikken Sekkei in 1959, Dr Maki has been involved in
various architectural projects, acting as Director and Deputy Principal at the
Osaka Office from 1981, Managing Director and Deputy Principal at the Osaka
Office from 1985, Senior Managing Director Corporate Planning and
Engineering from 1989. He taught at Kyoto University and Kyushu University
from 1981 to 1988. He has also served as a member of the Committee on
Environment and Energy of the Japan Association of Corporate Executives, and
as Vice Chairman of the Committee on Environment Conservation of Tokyo
Rotary Club. Dr Maki is a former board member of the Institute of Building
Energy Conservation and the Japan Facility Management Promotion
Association.

William A. McDonough, FAIA
William A. McDonough has been an international leader in sustainable
architecture since 1977. His design of the Environmental Defense Fund offices,
completed in 1985, helped launch the 'green building' movement in the USA.
His firm, William McDonough & Partners, have designed a number of award-
winning projects for such clients as Gap, Inc., Nike, Herman Miller, and Oberlin
College, and have set new standards for design quality, environmental
sensitivity and functional effectiveness. McDonough has written and lectured
extensively on his design philosophy and practice. He is the former Dean of the
School of Architecture at the University of Virginia and founded the
University's Institute for Sustainable Design. He has also been appointed the
A.D. White Professor-at-Large at Cornell University. He is the first and only
architect to receive the Presidential Award for Sustainable Development, the
nation's highest environmental honour, presented to him by President Clinton
in 1996.

Katashi Matsunawa, Registered Consultant Engineer
Born in 1944 and educated at the Graduate School of Waseda University,
Katashi Matsunawa is a Registered Consultant Engineer, Registered Engineer
of Building Services and currently Director at Nikken Sekkei Tokyo. He joined
Nikken Sekkei in 1970 and has been involved in many architectural projects,
such as the Shinjuku NS Building (1982); Tokyo Dome (1988); NEC Head Office
Building (1990); Tokyo Gas, Earth Port (1995) as an engineer in charge of HVAC
and sanitary installations design.

Part II Ten Green Buildings by Nikken Sekkei

Hisashi Yosano, JIA
Born in 1946 and educated at the Graduate School of Waseda University,
Hisashi Yosano is an architect and currently Managing Director at Nikken
Sekkei Osaka. Since joining Nikken Sekkei in 1971, he has designed various
projects, including: Hiroshima Art Museum (1978); International Institute for
Advanced Studies (1993); RITE Headquarters Building (1993).

Kiyoshi Sakurai, JIA
Born in 1950 and educated at the Graduate School of Kyoto University, Kiyoshi
Sakurai is an architect and currently Deputy Principal at Nikken Sekkei Tokyo.
Since joining Nikken Sekkei in 1976, he has been involved as a project architect
on such buildings as: Panasonic Multimedia Centre (1992); Konami Nasu
Seminar House (1995); Tokyo Gas, Earth Port (1996) and others. He also teaches
at Tokyo Metropolitan University.

Nobuhiro Tohmatsu, JIA
Born in 1945 and educated at the Graduate School of Kyoto University, Nobuhiro Tohmatsu is an architect and is currently Director at Nikken Sekkei. Since joining Nikken Sekkei in 1971, he has been involved in various projects including Osaka Municipal Central Gymnasium (1996); Department Store DAIMARU Kobe (1997); Kumamoto Prefectural General Sports Park Main Stadium (1998) as a project architect. He is also a lecturer at Kyoto University.

Shusaku Nanseki, JIA
Born in 1944 and educated at the Graduate School of Kyoto University, Shusaku Nanseki is an architect and currently General Manager, Design and Technical Department at Nikken Sekkei Nagoya. He Joined Nikken Sekkei in 1970, designing projects such as: Toyota Automobile Museum (1989); Aichi Prefectural Library (1991); and Kakegawa City Hall (1996) as a project architect. He is also a lecturer at Mie University.

Katsuya Kawashima, JIA
Born in 1957 and educated at the Graduate School of Kyoto University, Katsuya Kawashima is an architect and currently Design Principal, Design Department at Nikken Sekkei Osaka. He joined Nikken Sekkei in 1981. He has designed the following representative projects as a project architect: Kobe New City Hall (1989), Kobe Customs House (1999); and Lake Biwa Museum & UNEP International Environmental Technology Centre (1996).

Ataru Tsuchiya, JIA
Born in 1955 and educated at the Yamagata Technical High School, Ataru Tsuchiya is currently Senior Architect, Design Department at Nikken Sekkei Tokyo. He joined Nikken Sekkei in 1974. He has been involved in the following representative projects as a project architect: Meguro Gajyoen (1991), JICA Hokkaido International Centre (1996); and Times Square Building (1996).

Kazuya Ura
Born in 1947 and educated at the Graduate School of Tokyo National University of Fine Arts and Music, Kazuya Ura is an interior designer and currently President, Nikken Space Design Ltd. Since joining Nikken Sekkei in 1972, he has been involved in many projects including: Keio Plaza Hotel South Building (1980); Narita ANA Hotel (1989): and Izuna House (1991) as an interior designer.

Part III Research/Technical Essays

Masanori Shukuya, Dr Eng.
Born in 1953 and educated at the Graduate School of Waseda University, currently Dr Shukuya is a Professor at the Graduate School of Musashi Institute of Technology. He worked for Nikken Sekkei as an engineer from 1983 to 1985. Also he was a visiting scientist at Windows and Daylighting Group of Lawrence Berkeley Laboratory, the University of California from 1988 to 1989. Dr Shukuya is interested in the use of natural potentials to be found in our immediate exterior environment to condition luminous and thermal environment interiors, namely in daylighting, passive heating, passive cooling, and others. He was the recipient of the Paper Award of the Society of Heating, Air-conditioning and Sanitary Engineers of Japan (SHASEJ) in 1991. Also he is the author of *Light and Heat in the Built Environment* and *Seeking the Symbiotic Architecture* and others.

Shin-ichi Tanabe, Dr Eng.
Born in 1958 and educated at the Graduate School of Waseda University, currently Dr Tanabe is an Associate Professor in the Department of Architecture at Waseda University. He has also studied at the Laboratory of Heating and Air Conditioning of the Technical University of Denmark and at the Center for Environmental Design Research of the University of California, Berkeley. His research is centred on indoor environments related to the human body. Dr Tanabe was the recipient of the R. G. Nevins Award of ASHRAE in 1990.
He is also the author of *Indoor Chemical Pollution* and others.

Shuzo Murakami, Dr Eng.
Born in 1942 and educated at the Graduate School of the University of Tokyo, Dr Murakami is currently Professor at the Institute of Industrial Science, University of Tokyo. His research is focused on environmental control engineering for the built environment and urban technology based on both experimental techniques and numerical simulation. Recently he has been utilizing predictive methods using CFD (Computational Fluid Dynamics) based on mathematical models of turbulent flow. Dr Murakami is the recipient of the Best Paper Award from the Architectural Institute of Japan and SHASEJ. He is the author of *Architecture and Weather, Evaluation and Planning of Urban Air Flow Environment* and other works.

Akira Hoyano, Dr Eng.
Born in 1948 and educated at the Graduate School of the Tokyo Institute of Technology, Dr Hoyano is currently a Professor at the Graduate School of the Tokyo Institute of Technology. His research is focused on remote sensing, passive solar systems and green architecture. Dr Hoyano has been the recipient of the Best Paper Award from the Architectural Institute of Japan and from SHASEJ. He is the author of *Planning a Passive Solar House* and *Housing and Environment.*

Yoh Matsuo, Dr Eng.
Born in 1936 and educated at the Graduate School of the University of Tokyo, Dr Matsuo is a Professor at Meiji University and Professor Emeritus at the University of Tokyo. His research is focused on heat loads, air conditioner loads and planning for energy conservation in the built environment. Recently he has been proposing a sustainable design through heat transmission theory of urban environment. He is the recipient of the Best Paper Award from the Architectural Institute of Japan and from SHASEJ. Dr Matsuo is the author of *Energy Conservation of Built Environment* and *A Guide for Dynamic Heat Load Calculation of HVAC System*. He was a member of the Building Council for the Ministry of Construction, Government of Japan (1991–1999).

Tatsuo Inooka
Born in 1945 and educated at the Graduate School of Waseda University, currently Tatsuo Inooka is General Manager of the Environmental Engineering Group at Nikken Sekkei Osaka. His research is focused on the field of solar heating and cooling systems, heat storage, and simulation program development. Also he is the recipient of the International Best Paper Award from ASHRAE, and various awards from SHASEJ. He is the author of *Handbook of HVAC* and *Heat Burden Calculation Chart for the Design Architect.*

Koichi Kaiho
Born in 1955 and educated at Chiba University, Koichi Kaiho is currently Senior Engineer at Nikken Sekkei Tokyo. Since joining Nikken Sekkei in 1979, he has been involved in various types of architectural projects as a lighting system engineer. He was the recipient of the Lighting Design Award of Japan in 1989 for a Tokyo Dome project and the International Lighting Design Award in 1992 for the Toyota Auto Salon Amlux Tokyo. He is the author of *Encyclopedia of Lighting.*

Toshiharu Ikaga
Born in 1959 and educated at the Graduate School of Waseda University, currently Toshiharu Ikaga is an Associate Professor at the Institute of Industrial Science, University of Tokyo. He joined Nikken Sekkei in 1983 and worked on the lifecycle assessment of buildings and other similar projects until 1998. He created policies for environment-friendly architectural design guidelines for national and local governments, and also developed Environment Management Systems at Nikken Sekkei. He is the recipient of the Minister of Construction Award, Building Energy Saving Award, Technical Award from SHASEJ, and Best Paper Award from the 14th PLEA International Conference.

187

Photography and other credits
Fuminari Yamamoto, Hiroshi Shinozawa, Kaneaki Monma, Katsuyoshi Sawada, Kiyohiko Higashide, Koji Horiuchi, Mamoru Ishiguro, Masao Arai, Nacasa & Partners, Inc., Naotoshi Higuchi, Nagahiro Kobayashi, New Office Age Co., Ltd., Nikken Sekkei, Takao Onozato, RITE, Ryo Hata, Satoru Mishima, Seiji Kotaki, Shigeo Okamoto, Shinkenchiku-sha, SS, Takasaki Kenchiku, Shashin Kobou, Tokyo Gas, Toshio Kaneko, Yoshiharu Matsumura, Nagahiro Kobayashi, Remote Sensing Technology Center of Japan, The Kensetsu-Tsushin Shimbun Architecture, Construction & Engineering News (Daily), William A. McDonough and Partners, USA.

Illustrations
Stephanie Aaron: 15.3, 15.5a, 15.5b,15.6, 15.7, 17.7, 18.1,18.2, 18.3, 18.4, 18.5, 18.6, 18.7, 18.8
Thomas Cox: 2.13, 3.9, 3.10, 4.7, 5.13, 5.14, 5.16, 7.8, 7.19, 8.13, 10.14
Microcolor: 1, 2, 3a, 3b, 4, 5a, 5b, 6, 7a, 7b, 8, 9, 10, 11, 12, 13, 28, 29
Lloyd Miller: 11.1, 11.2a, 11.2b, 11.2c, 11.2d, 11.2e, 11.2f, 11.3a, 11.3b, 11.4, 12.1, 12.3, 12.4, 12.5, 12.8, 13.1a, 13.2a, 13.3a, 13.3b, 13.5b, 13.5c, 13.6, 13.10, 13.12, 15.1, 15.2a, 15.2b, 15.2c, 15.4, 16.1, 16.2, 16.3, 16.4, 16.5, 16.6a, 16.6b
Oliver Yourke: 2.7, 2.10, 2.11, 3.11, 3.12, 3.13, 4.6, 4.10, 4.11, 4.12, 6.9, 6.18, 6.19, 7.5, 7.7, 7.21, 9.6, 9.7, 9.14, 10.11, 10.12, 10.13

The Nikken Sekkei Approach to Green Buildings
1. Keeling D. et. al., (1989). Geophysical Monograph, vol. 55
2. IPCC (1995a). Climate Change 1995, The IPCC Second Assessment Synthesis of Scientific-Technical Information Relevant to Interpreting Article 2 of the UN Framework Convention on Climate Change
3. IPCC (1995b). *The Science of Climate Change*
4. OECD/IEA (1996). *World Energy Outlook, 1996 Edition*
5. Agency of Natural Resources and Energy (ed.) (1997). *Energy Statistics Synthesis,* Tsushosangyo-kenkyusha
6. International Energy Subcommittee, Advisory Committee for Energy (1995). *Interim Report—Asia Energy Vision*
7. Advisory Committee for Energy (1994). *Interim Report*
8. Environment Agency (1995). *Quality of the Environment in 1994*
9. GISPRI (ed.) (1998). Global Environment '98-99.

Chapter 11
1. Shukuya, M. (1994). Energy, Entropy, Exergy and Space Heating Systems. *Proceedings of the 3rd International Conference "Healthy Buildings '94", Vol. 1*, pp 369–374.
2. Shukuya, M (1996). Thermodynamic Consideration for Sustainable Architecture. *Proceedings of the 13th International Passive and Low Energy Architecture Conference*, Louvain-la-Neuve, 16–18 July 1996.
3. Shukuya, M. and Komuro, D. (1996). Exergy–Entropy Process of Passive Solar Heating and Global Environmental Systems. *Solar Energy*, 58:1-3, pp 25–32.
4. Shukuya, M. (1998). Bio-climatic design as rational design of exergy–entropy process. *Proceedings of the 15th International Passive and Low Energy Architecture Conference*, Lisboa, 1–3 June 1998.

Chapter 12
1. ASHRAE (1992). *ANSI/ASHRAE Standard 55-92R, Thermal environmental conditions for human occupancy.*
2. Fanger, P.O. (1970). *Thermal comfort*. Danish Technical Press.
3. *IS0-7730, Moderate Thermal Environments: Determination of the PMV and PPD indices and specification of the conditions for thermal comfort*. 1984.
4. Gagge, A.P. et. al. (1987). A standard predictive index of human response to the thermal environment, *ASHRAE Trans*. 93:1; pp 709–731.
5. Tanabe, S., Kimura, K. (1994). Effect of Air Temperature, Humidity, and Air Movement on Thermal Comfort Under Hot and Humid Conditions. *ASHRAE Trans*. 100: 2; pp 953–969.
6. Tanabe, S., Kimura, K. (1989). Importance of air movements on thermal comfort under hot and humid conditions. *ASHRAE Far East,* pp 95–103.
7. deDear, R., Brager, G.S. (1998). Developing an adaptive model of thermal comfort and preference. *ASHRAE Trans*.
8. Matsunawa, K., Iizuka, H., Tanabe, S. (1995). Development and Application of an Underfloor Air Conditioning System with Improved Outlet for a Smart Building in Tokyo. *ASHRAE Trans.* 101:2; pp 887–901.
9. Tanabe, S., Arens, E.A., Bauman, F.S., Zhang, H. (1994). Evaluating Thermal Environments by Using a Thermal Manikin with Controlled Skin Surface Temperature. *ASHRAE Trans*. 100:1, pp 39–48.
10. Nakano, J., Tanabe S. CIB
11. Tanabe, S., Suzuki, T., Kimura, K., Horikawa, S. (1995). Numerical Simulation Model for Thermal Regulation of Man with 16 Body Parts for Evaluating Thermal Environment (Part 1 Heat Transfer at Skin Surface and Comparison with SET* and Stolwijk Model). Architectural Institute of Japan, *Anthology of Technical Presentation Synopses*, August 1995, pp 417–418.
12. Tanabe, S., Yukinaka, S., Yoshida, H. (1997). Basic Study on Indoor Air Pollution HCHO and VOCs in Residential Buildings. *Review of Guidelines, Measurements and Evaluations in Europe and North America*. Anthology of technical papers presented to The Society of Heating and Air-conditioning and Sanitary Engineering of Japan, 1997, pp 49–52.
13. Mølhave, L., et. al. (1996). The Use of TVOC as an Indicator in IAQ Investigations. *Proc.INDOOR AIR '96* Vol. 2, pp 37–46.

14. Tanabe, S., Kimura, K. (1996). Comparisons of Ventilation Performance and Thermal Comfort among Underfloor, Displacement Ventilation, and Ceiling Diffuser Systems by Experiments in a Real Sized Office Chamber. *ROOMVENT 96,* pp 299–306.

Chapter 13
1. ASHRAE TRANSACTION 1995, Vol. 101 Pt2; pp 1144–1157.
2. Murakami, S., Ooka, R., Mochida, A., Yoshida, S., Kim, S. (1998). CFD Analysis of Wind Climate from Human Scale to Urban Scale. IWEF International Workshop on *CFD for Wind Climate in Cities*. 24–26 August 1998, Hayama, Japan, pp 44–62.

Chapter 14
1. Hoyano, A. (1996). *Environmental Science of the House.* The University of the Air Education Promotion Council.
2. Nakayama, H., Tanaka, S., Kan, Y. (1993). Geographical Observations on the Preparation of Global Nocturnal DMSP Images and Nocturnal Spectral Distribution. *The Journal of the Remote Sensing Association of Japan*, 13(4); pp 1–14.
3. Iino A., Hoyano A. (1996). Development of a method to predict the heat island potential using remote sensing and GIS data. *Energy and Buildings* 23; pp 119–205.

Chapter 15
1. Ministry of Construction (1993). *Handbook for Building Energy Saving Standards and Calculations*, Institute for Building Energy Conservation.
2. Matsuo, Y., et. al. (1988). *An Introduction to the Calculation of Dynamic Thermal Loads on Air Conditioning Systems.* Japan Building Mechanical and Electrical Engineers Association.
3. Architectural Institute of Japan (1988). *First Anthology of Building Design Documents: Environment.* Maruzen Ltd.
4. Architectural Institute of Japan (1981). *Planning of Building Energy Conservation.* Shokokusha Ltd.
5. Matsuo, Y., Maki E., Inooka, T. (1981). *Estimation Chart of Building Heat Load for Designers. Architectural Planning Based on the Energy Conservation Act.* Shokokusha Ltd.

Chapter 16
1. Matsuo, Y., Yokoyama, K., Inooka, T. (1985). *Energy Simulation of Air Conditioning Systems.* First report, 'Program outline and examination of calculation results'. Second report, 'Sub-system algorithms'. Third report, 'Functions of sub-system models'. Anthology of papers presented to the Society of Heating, Air Conditioning and Sanitary Engineering of Japan, pp 425–436.
2. Inooka, T., Matsuo, Y., Yokoyama, K. (1995). HASP/ACSS: Simulation Program for Energy Consumption of Air Conditioning Systems. Building Energy Simulation Conference Seattle, p187-194.
3. Air Conditioning System Simulation Research Group (1985). Comparison of Japanese Air Conditioning System Simulation Programs. *Japan Building Mechanical and Electrical Association,* 58:7; pp 65–78.
4. HASP/ACSS/8502 (1986). *Air Conditioning System-Standard Simulation Program. Program Instruction Manual.* Japan Building Mechanical and Electrical Engineers Association.

Chapter 17
1. Shirakawa, S., and others (1997). The Effect on Wakefulness of Exposure to Gradual Low Intensity Light Before Waking. Report from the 6th Japan Sleeping Environment Academic Conference.
2. Kaiho, K., and Matsunawa, K. (1995) Use of Digital Still Camera for Measurement of Luminance and Application to Light Environment Planning. *AIJ J. Technol. Des., No.1*, 229–232.

Chapter 18

1. Special Committee on Architecture and the Global Environment, AJJ (1992). *Impact of Buildings on the Global Environment.* Architectural Institute of Japan.
2. Sub-Committee on LCA, Committee on the Global Environment, AIJ (1997). *Evaluation of Building Design using Life Cycle CO$_2$ Analysis* (New Edition). Architectural Institute of Japan.
3. Sub-Committee on LCA guideline, Committee on the Global Environment (1998). *Draft LCA Guideline of Buildings.* Architectural Institute of Japan.
4. Ikaga, T. (1996). Reduction of Load on the Global Environment from Buildings. *Energy and Resources,* 17:5;
5. Japan Environmental Management Association for Industry (1998). *Practice of Life Cycle Assessment.*